ALMAGUIN

A Highland History

ALMAGUIN
A Highland History

ASTRID TAIM

NATURAL HERITAGE / NATURAL HISTORY INC.

Published by Natural Heritage/Natural History Inc. P.O. Box 95, Station O, Toronto, Ontario M4A 2M8

FIRST EDITION

Canadian Cataloguing in Publication Data

Taim, Astrid
Almaguin: A Highland History

Includes bibliographical references and index.
ISBN 1-896219-37-3

1. Almaguin Highlands (Ont,) — History. I. Title

FC3095.A447T34 1998   971.3'15 C98-931046.9
F1059.A44T34 1998

Cover and book design by Blanche Hamill, Norton Hamill Design
Edited by Jane Gibson

Cover background photo: A view of the Chikopi Falls on the Magnetawan River near the Knoepfli Inn on Highway 124, west of the village of Magnetawan.

Cover top photo: Time out from the barnraising. While the identification of the two women cannot be verified, it is believed that the woman on the left is Dora Michel of the South River area.

Cover bottom photo: See pg. 82

Frontispiece Photo: Loading logs on the Trout Creek Logging Railroad, 1915. This photograph was taken at the Wolf Lake Siding about four miles from the Mill. The men: Harry Reichstein, Jim Carr, Jake Eckensviler, and Harry Mechefski—running the jammer.

THE CANADA COUNCIL | LE CONSEIL DES ARTS
FOR THE ARTS | DU CANADA
SINCE 1957 | DEPUIS 1957

Natural Heritage/Natural History Inc. acknowledges the support received for its publishing program from the Canada Council Block Grant Program. We also acknowledge with gratitude the assistance of the Association for the Export of Canadian Books, Ottawa.

Printed and bound in Canada by Hignell Printing.

I thank my Mom for seeing me through this project, her great ideas—
and her unbelievable patience with me!

"No generation ever lived or worked under such pressure, or faced such complicated situations, as does the world today.

A humorist recently reminded us that our ancestors would wait quietly in a roadside inn for two or three days if they missed a stage coach.

We, on the contrary, squawk angrily if we miss the first section of a revolving door."

Powassan News, April, 1931

Acknowledgments

For their assistance and encouragement with research aspects of this project, I thank Peter Barr, the Publisher of the *Almaguin News* in Burk's Falls, Mary Johnston, also of the *Almaguin News*; Fred Heidman, General Manager of the *Parry Sound North Star* in Parry Sound, Lillian Rachar, also of the *Parry Sound North Star*; the staff of the West Parry Sound Library; the staff of the West Parry Sound Museum; Lela Daub, curator, Nipissing Township Museum in Nipissing Village; Tammy Robinson, archivist, Oshawa and District Historical Society; the staff of the Burk's Falls and District Museum in Burk's Falls, and Marilyn Raaflaub of the Magnetawan Museum. A special thank you goes out to Muriel Parker of Emsdale for allowing me the use of the photographs and historical data from the Tweedsmuire Village History (Emsdale-Scotia Women's Institute); to Pat Aitchison and Maryann Heinonen of the Perry Township Public Library in Emsdale for all their help, especially in tracking down the whereabouts of *Just One blue Bonnet* by Ada Florence Kinton, and to Christine (Niarchos) Bourolias, Reference Archivist of Special Collections, Archives of Ontario.

Because of the extensive research done for *Lake in the Hills, Strong Township and Sundridge: 1875-1925,* compiled by the late Patricia Lee and edited by Alice May Robinson in 1989, there was limited new information on the Village of Sundridge to be included in *Almaguin: A Highland History.* I gratefully acknowledge Mrs. Lee's hard work in bringing such a fine work to fruitation.

For their generosity in allowing me the use of photographs in their possession: Cecil Gilpin of Emsdale, Ron and Ethel Thorton, Marilyn (Bice) MacKay, all of Kearney; Betty Caldwell of Burk's Falls; the South River/Machar Union Public Library in South River; John (Jack) Trussler of North Bay, and David Plumb of Kendal for the photographs of Restoule. I also thank Jane Gavine of Burk's Falls, for lending me the wonderful *Cawthra Scrapbooks*; Harold Todd of Novar, Bud Leigh of Emsdale, John Lawson of Kearney and Vi Thomas of Burk's Falls for providing me with local history. I am also grateful to Peter Camani of Burk's Falls, Sandy Coombs of Magnetawan and Doug Mackey of Chisholm Township for speaking honestly about themselves; and for their wonderful anecdotes, the late Ralph Bice of Kearney and the late Elizabeth Marchant Maw-Cockeram of Toronto.

Special thanks to Dr. Jacke Phillips of the McDonald Institute for Archaeological Research at the University of Cambridge, UK, for being my friend all these years through thick and thin, to Mike McIntosh, for his endless enthusiasm and support of the project, and—to the bears themselves! Last, but not least, to my book publisher, Barry Penhale, for having faith in me—and to Heather Wakeling for her perseverance and dedication in preparing this manuscript for publication.

Contents

ALMAGUIN
A Highland History

Introduction

While the lumberjack toiled deep within the confines of the virgin forests, the real heros in the business were the river drivers. For most observers, it seemed a strange, romantic life these men led, always on the water. Since they followed closely behind the logs as the large booms on the Magnetawan River made their way downstream, their floating campsites were called 'cabooses.' And what majestic palaces they were! Large rafts adorned by roughly built sheds which contained a great wholesale stock of coarse provisions. Yes, the river drivers were the envy of all, their gypsy existence viewed as a colourful way of life although coarse and rough.

During the off-season, the men would pitch their canvas tents on a suitable spot along the river bank before heading for the closest town. Many a wooden sidewalk became deeply scarred from the sharp cleats in the soles of the river drivers' boots; these semi-annual visits to town were creating nothing but anxiety for the inhabitants. English artist and Salvationist, Ada Florence Kinton, who visited Burk's Falls in the spring of 1883, witnessed first hand the disparity between the river drivers and their temporary hosts. Her opinion was less than complimentary. "They're a fine-looking bunch of men, healthy, but a terribly bad lot, drinking appalling on land, and horrifying one with their talk. There have been a good many of them here at the hotel... ."

Florence Kinton was not alone in documenting this legendary lifestyle. Some years later and further down the river at the Village of Magnetawan, the crown timber agent for Parry Sound, Duncan F. MacDonald was to write, "The town is on a drunk. Shanty men and river rats clawing around."

It is unfortunate that relatively few written records have survived to provide a detailed account on what life must have been really like for those who ventured into this primitive wilderness during the last century. And in some cases, those that have documented stories that have been handed down, remain just that—a collection of stories many undated. But we are grateful to those who had the foresight to ensure that memories were recorded for posterity. Readers will be interested to know that rare documented local history on much of the region has been included in *Almaguin, A Highland History*. Late 19th century district weekly newspapers, including those from Toronto, periodicals and rarely seen published and unpublished community histories have greatly assisted in filling in the blanks on what little we know about Almaguin Highlands.

For example, in one of her many diaries, Ada Florence Kinton decided to document her one and only trip to Burk's Falls in the spring of 1883. Kinton had been staying with relatives in Huntsville during her four month stay in the area, producing watercolour sketches of the numerous little villages surrounding this thriving town. Her vivid description of this trip and the settlements she came across on her way north, is the only surviving record on the now almost forgotten community of Cyprus. Located just north of Novar, it had been a bustling settlement in her day. After her death, Kinton's diaries were collected together by her sister and published in Toronto in 1907.

The memoirs of pioneers-turned-writers,

such as E. J. Lawrence, Ernest Richardson, Hartley Trussler and Ralph Bice, have also proved invaluable, giving rare insight into the day to day struggles of the area settlers.

E. J. Lawrence's *Recollections of a Pioneer* remains the most accurate record available on the early days of Powassan and provide a vivid picture of what the community looked like then. The series ran in the *Powassan News* in the early 1950s, shortly before the writer's death.

Almaguin, A Highland History is about history in the making. In the final section personalities such as black bear specialist Mike McIntosh of 'Bear With Us' in Sprucedale and sculptor Peter Camani of Ryerson Township are just some of the people of Almaguin who are making a difference in their communities.

Almaguin, A Highland History is also about cross-country trail blazing. Today the Trans Canada Trail cuts through the heart of the Highlands along what has been described as the most novel section of the nation's 15,000 kilometre nature trail. Almaguin's contribution is the historic Rosseau- Nipissing Colonization Road which runs through the Village of Magnetawan and north towards Lake Nipissing.

Thanks to the foresight of businessmen in Magnetawan and South River the Discovery Routes Partnership was formed to reclaim this heritage roadway and others like it in the area and make them part of the national trail system. The Trans Canada Trail, which evolved out of Canada's 125th birthday celebrations, is the longest nature trail on earth and so designed to link the nation's provinces and territories together.

Almaguin, A Highland History takes a close look at the communities that blossomed along this government sponsored road, where as many as three stage coaches a day travelled north from Rosseau, carrying settlers up into the new territory. Communities such as Duf-ferin Bridge with its aspirations of city-status. That is, of course, until the day the railroad came... .

Some 80 kilometres north of the halfway point to the north pole and rising high above sea level, is a region that was once coveted for its game, silver birch and majestic white pine. Now known as the Almaguin Highlands, for centuries this area stretching up to the shores of Lake Nipissing was an unbroken forest that remained largely intact save where lakes, streams and beaver meadows punctured the forest floor to admit sunlight.[1] Relatively few written records have survived to provide any kind of detailed information on what life must have been like for those who came to this primitive wilderness. For this very reason the identities of many of the earliest explorers, and the settlers who followed them, remain unknown. And when government surveys commenced in the 1850s they were sporadic at best, with settlers not arriving in any great numbers until the end of 1860s when colonization roads were extended northwards. Before that time the travel choices for the very first settlers were exceedingly limited for accessing this new territory where they would stake their claim. Most of them came up the Champlain Trail from Pembroke, Arnprior and Ottawa.

When the first surveyors reached the Highlands, what lay before them was a 2,000 square-mile region which, in reality, was a communal hunting ground for Indian tribes. The Huron, Ojibwa, and Algonquin fished and hunted here on a regular basis without any apparent conflict. Although there are no actual records to substantiate the claim, it has been suggested that, for all intents and purposes, these tribes, very early on, had reached some sort of collective agreement to keep white explorers out of their traditional hunting areas. Consequently, so the suggestion goes, these explorers were led along the more accessible waterways that took them far away from Indian land. It appeared that nothing of much interest existed here for the white man and, for a while, the government seemed to be content to leave things as they were. In fact, during the early 1860s there were thoughts of turning the whole area into an Indian reservation.

That is, until the lumbermen came...

The tranquility offered by this solid stretch of forest was soon shattered by the omnipresent sawmill. The Ontario Free Grants & Homestead Act had new territory to conquer and time was money. By the late 1860s, the Magnetawan District as it was then called, found settlers pushing their way north past Huntsville to stake land claims. The demand for building materials grew. In record time there were so many sawmills set up between Bracebridge and North Bay that they were actually within hearing distances of one another. Railway ties and pulpwood scows plugged the waterways, competing for space with the steamships. Soon the magnificent forest north of Huntsville was eaten away, "Replaced by the everlasting vision of shingles and shingle bolts, staring back at one at every turn."[2]

1 | Settling the New Land

Nestled within the chain of steamboat lines connecting the lake system, which included Fairy, Mary and Vernon lakes, was the Huntsville of 1870. Of course, it didn't have an official name just yet. The settlement was still in the process of being carved out of the thick encircling forest and consisted of little more than one so-called street.[1] In 1862 the town site for this picturesque village was picked out by a hunter and trapper named William Cann. A short time later he built a log shanty ontop of a hill right in the middle of the new settlement. As it turned out that shanty was to outlast Cann's stay, for just one year later Cann disposed of his claim and went back to trapping. The shanty was still there in 1892, presumably taken over by another settler.[2] The community experienced little growth over the next few years; there were no sidewalks, no street lighting and few of the comforts of civilization. Water traffic was frequent, but walking on foot through the settlement was another matter. Pedestrians who did venture onto the street had to do so at their own risk, for it meant finding a path that avoided the carcasses of dead horses, manure everywhere and mounds of garbage. And to top it all off, the unlucky man or woman on foot also had to contend with a wade through the mud. According to one scribe from the times, the mud, "Why, It would have honoured an Indian village in the camp of Jacques Cartier."[3]

In spite of these early primitive living conditions, by the 1870s the settlement was to flourish under the Ontario Free Grants & Homestead Act. Ideally situated following the windings of the Muskoka River, the community looked out from the hilltops over lovely lakes, lying mirror-like on every side, near and far. And best of all, the air was exhilarating, fresh and pure.[4] The new settlement even had a printing office open up in 1875, the *Huntsville Liberal*. And just a few rods (11 yards) away from the newspaper office, a militia man from Montreal was to make history by constructing the first permanent home.[5] Captain George Hunt had made his first trip to the new community alongside the Muskoka River in 1863. According to one report, Hunt and a Mr. E.G. Hilditch were the ones who acquired Cann's land claim.[6] However, the Captain apparently went back to Montreal and it was not until 1869 that he decided to take advantage of Ontario Free Grants & Homestead Act and made his return trip a permanent one.

By the time Captain George Hunt had become the first storekeeper and post master, the 'free grant boom' had taken hold. Arriving shortly after Hunt were Allan Shay, Fred Shay, George Lassiter, and George and

In the winter, the settler's shanty almost appeared as if it was snuggling up to the snowdrifts for warmth.

The first challenge a settler faced in the new territory was building a shelter from the elements. This typical log house in the woods was a familiar sight throughout the area during the earliest years of settlement. By constructing the shanty out of logs, the pioneer also got a start at clearing the land.

Nathan Norton, all of whom settled either in the village or on adjacent farms.[7] As Hunt had done before them, they eventually sent for their families, but early records fail to identify them. Seemingly it was by pure coincidence that the name 'Huntsville' was chosen for the new settlement. Although there had been others, such as William Cann, through the area before him, they fell into the category of a transient population. In most cases, new settlements were named after the rich and powerful in the community, but this was not the case here. The captain's bark-roof shanty may have been modest, but its occupants were there to stay, so the name stuck. As the Huntsville area continued to attract more and more settlers, the time came to push northwards into a whole new wilderness area. A wilderness that eventually became known as the Almaguin Highlands.

2 | **The Unknown**

It is a great loss to local history that the early inhabitants did not keep any real records of what went on and by whom, in the beginning days of settlements in Almaguin. Occasionally one comes across some isolated cases, such as stories telling where a man had carved out a home in the wilderness, but unfortunately there are no names and no dates provided to document the claim.

This first story is a case in point. The man's great grandfather had walked many miles through the bush, leaving his family behind. He searched and searched until he found the ideal spot which just happened to be in Perry Township. In true pioneer fashion he then proceeded to build a log shanty in readiness for the arrival of his wife and family, who were awaiting his summons. Apparently temporarily lodged in a settlement some thirty miles away, their only way to reach the new home was on foot.[1]

Judging by when the story was first told, the age of the story-teller and by adding three generations to that, it would suggest an approximate time of 115 years ago (and from our current year this would be about 136 years ago). Using this as a reference point, it would have to be accepted that the mystery pioneer's trek into Perry Township took place around 1862.[2] But who was this man? Where did he come from? Who did he send to get his family and furthermore, in the end, what happened to them all? And who was the original story-teller? A descendent of the family perhaps, but we will never know as today their names remain just as much a mystery as the name of the pioneer.

Another such tale evolved during the building of the Rosseau-Nipissing Colonization Road through the Parry Sound District. Despite the back breaking work, the road gangs found time for humour, most of it harmless. Again, no dates or names were ever provided to support the story. This particular event involved two Irish teamsters working on a section of the colonization road outside of the Village of Magnetawan. Both men apparently had identical names. But as it turned out, they were not related to one another, unless one wishes to say that all Irishman are related by the mere fact that they are Irish. Both worked under the same foreman and were not in any way adverse to having a little fun with their boss.

The day came when a large rock had to be removed from the roadbed and a team was needed to carry out the work. While both men were heading away from the foreman for a fresh load of gravel from a nearby pit, the foreman called out their name. The duo immediately turned their horses around, much to the consternation of the foreman who then attempted to explain exactly which man he needed to do the work. In the midst of the explanation, the teamsters both turned around again and headed back towards the gravel pit. He was left scratching his head to figure out if he would ever get the best of the two Irishmen, but the day did come when the foreman got the last laugh.

It was nightfall by the time one of the teamsters got around to heading back towards camp. Crossing paths with a skunk, he startled it and paid dearly for the unfortunate encounter. When he later arrived at the camp, the rest of the men refused to allow him anywhere near the place until he 'smelled like a rose, an Irish rose that was.' From that moment on, the teamster was nicknamed 'Rosy,' a name that apparently stayed with him for life. The foreman's luck had changed and life made much easier for the duration of road construction.[3]

There are always difficulties when probing into the uncharted past, in separating fact from fiction. Nothing more so than unravelling the tale behind the name of the Distress River in Chapman Township. One such tale uncovered from the early settlement days, involved a number of men who lost their lives while eating a meal on the banks of this river. As the story goes, the party in question, in making a cup of tea to go with their meal, used the water right from the river. Nobody noticed that as the water was being poured into the kettle, a black lizard found its way into the container—one very poisonous lizard in fact. Subsequently the tea was brewed, lizard and all, with the deadly venom being released in the heat. The entire crew, having drunk the beverage, were to die an agonizing death within several hours. Thus the name "Distress" for this particular river. Another less serious tale retrieved from the past was that several surveyors while charting the area around the river ran out of food. For several days they were in "Distress."[4]

In the olden days, the hotels in most villages were of frame construction, as were the majority of the buildings. The main source of heat, particularly in the winter time, was from huge pot-bellied stoves, kept going around the clock in order to warm the many guest rooms. The Village of Sundridge had three such hotels at one time, Jackson's, Aldjon's, and the Queen's Hotel, the latter operated by James Herget. Two of the hotels were in existence before 1895 and were destroyed by fire in the years between 1891 and 1902. The records unfortunately fail to clearly state which two hotels burned and which one was spared.

One very cold night in February, the temperature dropped to 20 degrees F below zero, with a strong bitter north wind beating down on the shivering inhabitants of the Village of Sundridge. Since it was impossible to keep the upstairs rooms of any hotel at the time even reasonably comfortable, a couple of travellers at one of the Sundridge establishments, fed up with their freezing quarters, left their cold rooms to gather and sleep around the big woodstove in the sitting room of their hotel. It was shortly before daybreak when they were awakened by the tramping feet of a lumberjack. Standing before them was truly a spectacle of a man—his whiskers festooned with icicles, his nose nipped with frost, his eyelashes fringed with his frozen breath. Among those who had spent the night huddled around the stove, was one John Maxwell, a former employee of Edgar's store in Sundridge. Always ready with his Irish wit, John looked up and said, "My goodness, man! What room were you in last night!"[5]

The Great North Road starting from Parry Sound was to become one of the more important transportation routes. Up until 1866, there had been little attention paid to a northerly route from this village. It soon became clear that in order to encourage settlers to move deeper into the new territory, away from the more accessible and readily settled areas, a road had to be constructed to intersect with the Rosseau-Nipissing Colonization Road. Providing easier access to Lake Nipissing and points north was the prime motivation for the government in building a route for the anticipated rush of wagon trains.

By 1870 this new road meandered out and up through the community of McKellar, through Hagerman Township into Croft Township and ultimately to Ahmic Harbour. An unnamed woman settler described it as a "vital link between Parry Sound and some of the most beautiful country in the north."[6] Unfortunately, all that is left of these first eye-witness accounts are fragmented excerpts out of the 1876 and 1877 diaries which belonged to this settler. Past researchers, however well intentioned, in recording her recollections for posterity chose to obscure the identity of the woman, leaving us to wonder as to her fate.

Fueled by vague promises made by government officials, many hundreds of people, mostly English and German, set out to transform the vast tracts of virgin forest of central Parry Sound in the last century. This particular English woman travelled to Spence Township from Parry Sound with her husband, two sons and one daughter. From the few entries written by her that have survived, one gets a tiny glimpse of what the typical homesteader saw as they journeyed the last miles to the promised land. In an attempt to make the recorded diary entries anonymous, the family name, the names of the husband and children, unfortunately were omitted by the previous researcher.

What is clear is that the woman's diary was apparently meant for her sister back in England, as the writings appear as letters to her that describe not only the daily household routine, but the breathtaking beauty of the countryside as the seasons changed.

'Dear Sis.
As I write, the snow is falling and making the trees very majestic. I promised to describe our trip by stage from the Village of Parry Sound to our new home. Well, I shall keep my promise, but not all at once, as I feel that one cannot describe its full beauty in one short letter.

We hope that the children will learn to appreciate the beauty of their new home. To call it a spot of heaven on earth I do not think could be misconstrued as sacrilegious.

The stately maples, now bare, are forced to take second place by the tall kingly pines, whose aroma is ever stimulating. I am sure, dear sister, that your health would improve if you were to join us here...

As you are aware from my last letter, we have now been here nearly two months, but if I live to be a 100, I shall never forget the array of colour that greeted us on our trip. Indeed, I have seen many masterpieces of colour, painted by famous artists, but believe me my dear sister, God is still the greatest artist of them all. He spared not one colour in His vast repertoire.

...to the pine, but this was not the case when... [maple] had been touched by frost and the leaves had taken on different colours from gold to blood red and all the possible, and perhaps impossible, shadows in between.

Those stately trees reach their branches over the road as if to have a more personal contact with their neighbours across the street. To ride or walk between this avenue of colour makes one feel as if their life is receiving an additional blessing from the Almighty. I believe that nowhere else in the world can you find such beauty to describe it, I feel, can at best only give a very inadequate picture.

To be able to appreciate the beauty of trees, sparkling brooks and majestic waterways, one must see them.

As much as I love the home land (*England*), I have come to love this vast land of Canada even more...

"My Dear Sis,
The children and I have taken time off to go for one of our many walks in Mother Nature's Garden. There are literally millions of wild flowers that appear to be trying to appear even more beautiful than their neighbours.

Early this morning, my husband took our oldest son and they went fishing for trout. They had their usual good luck, returning with seven of the prettiest fish you could imagine. It's almost a shame to take such beautiful creatures from the water, however, I believe that the Almighty has placed them there for our use, and use them I must. They must be cleaned and salted in preparation for the evening meal.

My husband and son could have caught more without difficulty, but they knew that seven would amply feed our family for one meal. My husband has little patience with people who waste God's provisions.

Tomorrow we are hoping to have the reverend for one of his most welcome visits.

I shall ask my husband to get some more of those lovely trout, as I know the reverend likes them so well.

The boys and I have the garden prepared for planting and we shall shortly plant our winter vegetables. My husband has promised to make what he terms as a root cellar, in which he feels the vegetables will keep without freezing.

This is the only thing I do not like about this country, the extreme cold temperatures. It is not unusual for one to freeze one's face or feet should they be unduly exposed to the extreme temperatures. I wish to hasten to say, my dear sister, that although one may experience a certain discomfitures at such times, the winter is most invigorating. I have yet to have a cold since being here and you know how I suffered from this malady.

The candles are getting low, I must get busy an make some more, but I am going to use this as an excuse to continue this letter tomorrow...

I have just finished the candles that I spoke about yesterday, I have also set bread. My, how it makes a woman's heart leap for joy when she sees her husband and family sit down and devour two large loaves of bread fresh from the oven, to say nothing of the buns that I make as a special treat when I bake bread.

I always try to find some kind of fruit to put into those buns. My, those boys of ours give their father a run for his money when it comes to those fruit buns.

Sometime soon a new dress must be made for our daughter. My, how that child grows. This evening I must start some winter socks for my men."[7]

The writings clearly demonstrate that this English settler was an educated woman who was not afraid of taking on the challenge of making a home in the wilderness with her husband and children. It is truly unfortunate that their identity may never be known.

To get to Spence Township where the family staked its claim, the family travelled the Great North Road across the territory in a north-west direction towards the Village of Magnetawan. It is interesting to note that Spence Township is located south of the village and the Rosseau-Nipissing Colonization Road cuts right through it in a south-north direction.

Love and marriage hurdled some rather unbelievable barriers in the early days. Reverend John Garrioch, who oversaw the building of St. Andrew's Presbyterian Church in Burk's Falls during his incumbency from 1886 to 1888, had also been stationed at Powassan for some time.[8] A certain young couple thought he was still in the northern Almaguin community and one day walked eleven miles only to find that their minister had since left. They were informed that Reverend Love, a superannuated minister, lived at Trout Creek and might just be able to help, so they decided to walk the rails another six or so miles and get hitched down there.

Just how long it took the lovers to cover the distance both ways, one can only speculate, but the knot was tied. The ordeal was by no means over as there was more for this determined couple to overcome. In fact, the honeymoon trip turned out to be rather hectic and unique. On their return, they were caught in a thunderstorm about midway between Trout Creek and Powassan. There was no shelter between the rails. It must have been a terrifying experience for the newlyweds, whoever they were.[9]

Sometimes, what you see, is what you get, no fabulous supporting tale. One such case involves a small settlement located two miles southeast of Nipissing Village called Christian Valley. Someone once made an inquiry as to the origin of the name and the answer was— it was believed a Christian once had passed through the area.

The following poem was submitted by Lottie Wraight of Newton, New Jersey to the *Almaguin News*, August 17, 1967. Mrs. Wraight wrote that she recognized the poem as being about Christian Valley, the community she grew up in during the turn of the century. Unfortunately, she failed to mention where she found the poem.

CHRISTIAN VALLEY

"From Riek's Rock to Simpson's Hill
and Aultman's Rock above the rill,
The Valley lay all in between,
With towering trees of vivid green.

Pioneers they came from Parry Sound
Through the bush and dale and over mounds,
Flour and bacon in their blankets rolled,
And oft it rained and they were cold.

Across their backs was also slung
Their clothes and axe and hunting gun.

From Germany that land of fame,
To railway's end at Pembrook came,

To hue a home from the forest green.
The Valley was an answered dream;
The trees were cut and a clearing made
And timbers for a home were laid;

The shanty walls were chinked with moss
For these pioneers were never at a loss,
To use materials at hand;
The door was hung with a withen band,

A roof of cedar scoops was made,
One side up the other down, were laid
To shed the rain and wind and storm,
In coldest winter would be so warm.

With winter gone the slashes blazed,
And high in the tree-tops as we gazed
The spruces roared in fiery flames
And billowing smoke spread or the plains.

Rain on the dying embers fell
The ashes leached out the potash good
    and well;
Oats, wheat and turnips seeded here;
With a rooted fence to keep the deer

And rabbits, or the prowling bear
From taking over much his share
Our staple food for the coming year.
The Masons, Smiths and Knotts entwined

And at Riek's Rock were the German Klines,
Frank Croteau of French descent
To make a homestead he was bent,
And settled just across from knott.

A home the Armstrongs they had sought
Built near the rapids on a lot;
Simpsons topped the western hill.
Their stalwart sons worked with a will

To plant an orchard on the hillside sand,
And grew the finest apples of the land.
Hartley and his four Bernardo boys
    built down the hill
With Orton's shanty just above the rill;

The Rowlandsons with glee did find
Their many acres were free grant land.
All these families kept in touch
They worshipped in everyday of toil,

As nature unfolded from the soil;
The Golden Rule, love one another,
Truly they were Christian brothers.
God in his Heaven shone down from above

Poured out his blessings of health and love;
Coming together at one of their bees.
Eating their dinner under the trees
Said one to another, there must be a name

We've all been so busy no one's to blame;
A name we must have for this Valley so fair
For though our faiths differ our God is
     the same
So Christian Valley was the name it became. "

Another story from early settlement days of this area involved a student who had been sent back to the village of Restoule by his church. Now, no one knows if this could have been the same Christian. All that is known for certain is that the young man was said to have come across a cabin consisting of just three walls and a blanket. He was greeted by a rather slovenly young woman who promptly sat down on the bare ground. The student paused for a moment before introducing himself and asking if there were any fresh meat available.

Looking up at him, the woman replied without hesitation, "Well, I don't know, but Pa shot something a week ago and its hide is a hanging in the cow shed."[10]

The history of Almaguin is as diverse as the region it covers and its people a hardy lot, a fact to which the local newspapers from the late 19th century and early 20th century frequently attest. A few of those early district weeklies which managed to survive the ravages of time, reveal lively accounts of community activities, penned by the newspaper correspondents that appeared to have scoured the countryside. And readers were assured that the news they were reading, was "Supplied from the raciest and most reliable sources and up to the very latest dates."[11]

3 | John Sampson Scarlett

Keeping just one step ahead of the rest of the settlers along the Muskoka Colonization Road were John Sampson Scarlett and his young brother, Robert Colin Scarlett, two enterprising brothers from Northern Ireland. While John was to become one of the best known storekeepers in the early settlement of the districts of Muskoka and East Parry Sound, he also was a key figure in the formation of new Anglican parishes in the region.

It appears that the Scarletts were a family of some means and, coming to Upper Canada in the early 1860s from Londonderry with their mother Elizabeth (nee Sampson) and sister Elizabeth, the brothers quickly took advantage of the opening of new territory for settlement. Upon arrival they set to building log stores in Gravenhurst, Uffington, Bracebridge, Utterson and Port Sydney.[1] The eldest of the three brothers, Thomas, had arrived in the colony long before the rest of the family and eventually rose to the rank of Lieutenant T. Scarlett of Cobourg, Canada West.

With Robert running the draying business, hauling goods from Washago northwards to the various stores, John operated the other businesses by himself. Known as the Scarlett Bros. of Utterson, the brothers eventually opened a branch store in Huntsville, locating it on the south side of the Muskoka (colonization) Road. Using his astute business sense, John Scarlett waited until after 1870, when the construction of a bridge across the Muskoka River was completed, so he could become the first merchant to open a store west of the bridge.[2] It was in this modest general store built out of logs in 1872, that the Anglican parish would hold its first church services in the community with Scarlett's full support.[3]

A few years after the Huntsville store was up and running with a manager hired to oversee it, John and his wife, Maria Fetterley, the daughter of United Empire Loyalists John Peter Fetterley and Nancy Fetterley (nee Hanes), moved on to the next settlement. As always, Scarlett immediately settled down to the business of building a general store, this time in a tiny community on the hill. According to local rumour, Maria's nickname was 'Em' and upon her death, a short while after the Scarletts arrived, the village site became known as Emsdale. Now a widower left with five small children, John Scarlett saw no reason to linger on and, gathering his small family together, continued his push northwards.

But before he left he hired Alex Thom to run the Emsdale store in his absence, along with the post office.[4] Thom resided in nearby Katrine, where he ran a farm and at one point during the 1870s, taught school as well. However, as enthusiastic as he was at first over being the manager of the local general store, he didn't see himself remaining a storekeeper forever. Eventually he seized the opportunity, in 1893, to purchase the weekly newspaper, the *Sundridge Echo* from R. Hewitt. Initially, deciding to print the publication in Katrine, Alex Thom took on a partner, John Harper. Soon after Harper and Thom, with his wife Sarah and their two daughters Agnes and Ruby, along with the newspaper, moved north to Sundridge. To his immense pleasure, Harper married into the family, taking Ruby, as his wife. The newlyweds moved to a little house on Barrie Street near the lake.[5] For the rest of his life, Alex Thom never strayed far from the newspaper, writing for the *Echo* until his death in 1914. He always knew he had made the right decision in leaving Scarlett's store in Emsdale.

Throughout Scarlett's life, men such as Alex Thom who knew him however briefly, continued on with their lives long after he'd gone, involving themselves in making their own fortunes in the new territory. Scarlett, in the meantime, continued on his quest, building a succession of stores to service the settlers coming up to the north. In Burk's Falls, he was able to pool his resources with James Sharpe, another newcomer from the Huntsville area, who had decided by 1881, to take up permanent residence in the village. Together, they built a brand new general store.[6]

Predictably, Scarlett's restless nature soon had him moving on. The new business venture apparently did not hold Sharpe's attention for long either, and a local man by the name of William Copeland was hired to manage it. Eventually Sharpe made the decision to sell the business to Louis E. Kinton of Huntsville.[7] By the close of the 1880s, John Scarlett's travels had taken him all the way to Nipissing Village, an area accessible only by water and portage, as Gravenhurst was still the 'end of steel.' It remains a wonder how John Scarlett managed delivery of the community's first piano, as there are no records left that documented the feat.[8]

Because of its crucial water links, Nipissing quickly grew to be known as the 'Hub of the North.' As well, the provincial government's Crown Lands Office was located here. Ultimately the village was incorporated in 1888.[9] Unfortunately, this was to be a short lived success story for the community. By the fall of 1889, the Pacific Junction Railway finally had pushed northwards. Aubrey White, the assistant commissioner of Crown Lands, began the critical transfer of his Nipissing operation east to Powassan, the government's newly chosen train stop. John Scarlett, ever aware of opportunities, purchased Tom Gorman's old store on Mill Street in Powassan, only to turn around and offer it as a temporary home for the Crown Lands Office. He then went on to build what would be his last store that was to house both the government agency and his beloved general store. It was here in the upstairs living quarters that his daughter Kathleen was born to his second wife, Millie Maud Scott. It is unfortunate that historians of the time neglected to give much thought to recording Millie's contribution to the community before her marriage. Today little is known of where she came from or who she was.

While the Crown Lands office was being relocated, John S., as he was nicknamed, assisted in the moving of government documents by driving a team and buggy over the Bellu and Quigley hills, morning and night, to and from Nipissing. It was during one of these trips that his horses were spooked and John Scarlett had much difficulty calming them. Searching for the cause of his team's fright, he spotted a yoke of unbroken oxen not far from the road, one of which had its front foot twisted over the yoke, which somehow had slipped. This malady, referred to as 'turning the yoke,' apparently was caused by the animals swinging their 'nether ends' outward.[10]

Scarlett immediately reported the matter to Quigley, the owner of the oxen. The old man said he was willing to trade them for a quiet horse, but first, someone else would have to catch them as the oxen didn't like him particularly. Once he arrived back in Powassan, Scarlett passed the word on to a William Lawrence, who went that very same evening to find the oxen at Quigley's place. After staying the night, Lawrence caught and roped the oxen, a task being made easier by the steer twisted in the yoke having a very sore leg. Lawrence gave Quigley a horse, harness and plow in exchange for the oxen, yoke and two new draft chains. He claimed they were the hardest pair of steers to break that he ever had worked with, but they served their purpose at the time.[11]

About the same time of John Scarlett's arrival in Nipissing, a man in his fifties who went by the name of 'Charles White,' appeared. At first, keeping to himself and living at a distance from everyone else, the stranger eventually moved into a rough shanty on the Scarlett property in Nipissing. There he spent most of his time in solitude, hoeing potatoes. One Fall day, two American detectives, accompanied by a Gravenhurst constable, arrived at the shanty. Upon hearing his right name being called, the individual attempted to flee, but the detectives seized their man and shackled him.

To the surprise of many, it was revealed that 'Charles White,' who had kept to himself all this time, was a wanted fugitive, a murderer, who had been on the lam for some time. It had been back in the 1870s that this American had murdered his wife in Indiana and disposed of the body by burning it. A short time later he killed a man and attempted to dispose of this body in the same fashion. Escaping from prison, 'White' first had made his way to California, then north into Canada and eventually to the wilds of the Parry Sound area. What gave him away? It is said that an envelope addressed to his brother written in his own handwriting, led to his detection.[12]

John Sampson Scarlett died on April 29, 1909 and was buried in Powassan, many miles away from Huntsville where he had supported the holding of the first Anglican service in his general store. His legacy, however, would live on through the area as Scarlett is regarded as the founder of Powassan's St. Mary's Anglican parish where his wife, Millie Maud, eventually became the organist at the church.

His descendants include a great-granddaughter, Stuart (Pat) Lindsay of Port Sydney,

from his first marriage through his only son, Thomas. From Scarlett's second marriage came a grandson, Stan Darling, who rose from the ranks of local politics to eventually become the M.P. for Parry Sound/Muskoka. He not only won, but retained the seat for the Conservative Party in 1972 and went on to hold the riding until his retirement.[13]

Darling's amazing political track record was first profiled back in the 1950s, by Toronto's CFRB. The station's, 'Ontario Marches On,' showcased communities and personalities from across the province, much like today's CBC television's 'On The Road Again.' Sponsored by Cities Service Oil Company, the program aired three times a week, at 6:15 p.m. on Mondays, Wednesdays and Fridays. This is what the program had to say about Stan Darling, as reprinted in the *Burk's Falls Arrow and Sundridge Echo*, Thursday, March 1, 1951.

'1951 marks Reeve Stan Darling's 11th consecutive year on the village council (Burk's Falls) and his fifth consecutive term as Reeve. In all 11 years, he has yet to contest an election, having received acclamation each year.

Mr. Darling is a young man, 39, an insurance agent, with his business through the district. He is aggressive and fights hard in the interests of the people who have put him in office, and he, with his councillors, have been responsible for many of the community's improvements in recent years. He is a past-president of the local Lions Club, and an international counsellor of the Lions' International Organization, and served as district-governor in 1947-48 for District A-5, which covers Northern Ontario and part of Quebec.

He is very interested in and very active in all community affairs and in addition to his position as reeve, he is also president of the Burk's Falls Agricultural Society and a district director of the Agricultural Societies of Ontario, and president of the Parry Sound Municipal Association. Reeve Darling is a member of the United Church of Canada and is a Scottish Rite Mason.

He was born in Callander, but has been well known in Burk's Falls for over 20 years. He is married and in addition to his wife, Mona, his family consists of his two sons, John 8, and Peter 5.'

Stan Darling retired from federal politics in July 1993 and still resides in Burk's Falls.

4 | The Scotia Junction Difficulty

Trains don't stop here anymore. They haven't in years. All the rails and ties have been taken up and the railbed is but a ridge of gravel stretching across the countryside. If you happen to glance east across the swamp, you will see the odd building left here and there along the CN line. Scotia Junction is located south of Emsdale and sandwiched between Highway 592 to the east and Highway 11 to the west. Sadly, not much remains of the village that, ninety years ago, was the railroad centre of the north.

Oddly enough, the swamp itself is a testimonial to Scotia Junction's former greatness. Between the years 1873 and 1879, Perry Township was surveyed by David Gilruth and William Slorach. At one point, Slorach chose the shores of a shallow lake for his homestead, only to have Grand Trunk officials decide the lake was in the way of their railroad. They went about blasting the rock at the head of Ragged Falls, thereby draining the lake. Slorach's homestead ended up sitting on the edge of a marsh instead of a lake.[1]

By 1885 the Grand Trunk Railway from Toronto to North Bay had pushed into the area and Scotia was born. Three years later, lumber baron J.R. Booth decided to build his own railway from Ottawa and Arnprior to Parry Sound, to provide a more direct transportation system across the Great Lakes and on to the Ottawa and Montreal areas. Construction was begun from both ends and in 1896 the lines joined at the western boundary of Algonquin Park. Along the way Booth had some luck on his side. In 1885 a group of citizens in Parry Sound had incorporated a private railway scheme in order to build a line from a point on the Northern and Pacific Junction Railway (by now part of the Grand Trunk Railway) at or near Burk's Falls to Parry Sound.[2] By 1892 the Parry Sound Colonization Railway Company, the formal name of the group, received government permission to change its proposed intersection with Northern and Pacific Junction Railway, from Burk's Falls to Scotia Junction. This change was granted in anticipation of Booth's westward advancing line.[3] As was his style, and without any warning, Booth seized an opportunity to acquire this company and, on December 20, 1896, the first train on the Ottawa Arnprior Parry Sound Railway ran from Depot Harbour to Ottawa.[4] Thousands of cores of tanbark acquired from the large stands of hemlock, east and west of Scotia Junction, now waited in anticipation for shipment to Boston and other eastern centres. There were also millions of board feet of the choicest pine lumber waiting to be loaded at stops in Whitehall and Kearney.[5] Scotia became Scotia Junction and the crossroads of two great railways.

The 'old man,' as J.R. Booth was called, was becoming a legendary figure in the Canadian lumbering industry. Almost single-handedly, he built an empire of sawmills, railways and canals. Booth, known for not taking anything on unless there was a big profit in it for him, primarily built the Ottawa Arnprior Parry Sound Railway to ship his lumber to his mills. Booth's parents had immigrated from Ireland early in the century and started farming at Lowes near the village of Waterloo (Shefford County) in the Eastern Townships of Quebec.

The second railway station at Scotia Junction. Built in 1914, it was a far cry from the one it replaced.

Scotia Junction once was one of the most important railroad towns in Ontario and the architecture of its' first rail station reflected this importance. In 1895 the Grand Trunk Railway (GTR) from Toronto to North Bay was built and Scotia was born. That same year, lumber baron J.R. Booth completed his railroad between Ottawa and Parry Sound and Scotia became the 'junction' of the GTR and the Canada Atlantic Railway. The years 1885 to 1919 were the heydays of this busy railroad town. In 1914 the Scotia Junction railway station burned to the ground, to be replaced by a generic building.

John Rudolphus Booth was born April 5, 1827, one of six children.[6] At the age of 20, he left home and went up the Ottawa Valley to work in the lumber camps. As early as the 1850s, American lumber operations were in full swing in the area and Booth set about to learn everything he could from them. Before long, he set up his own shingle mill at Chaudiere Falls on the Ottawa River at Bytown, later renamed Ottawa. Steadily, he began to acquire timber limits along the upper river and in a few years, his holdings had spread away up the Madawaska Valley into Algonquin Park, and on up to Parry Sound and Nipissing districts. Building a railway became his ultimate dream.[7] That railway eventually became the Canada Atlantic Railway and, by 1899, had taken under its corporate umbrella, a series of sections in the rail system previously known by their own incorporated names.[8]

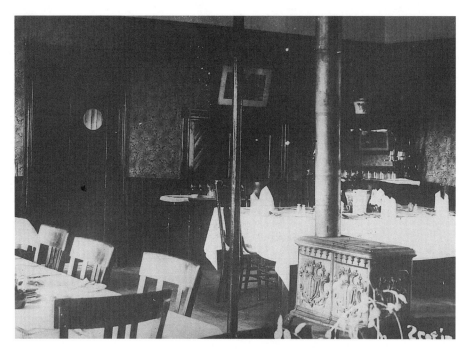

Hotel patrons were treated in style while stopping at Scotia Junction. White linen tablecloths and linen napkins gave an air of civility to the main dining room.

As the junction of the Grand Trunk (GTR) and the Canada Atlantic Railway lines (Ottawa to Depot Harbour), Scotia Junction's prominence as railroad town continued to grow rapidly. The community became known far and wide from Toronto to North Bay and from Parry Sound to Montreal. However, its significance as the cross roads for the province's two major rail lines did not mean that all was well in Scotia Junction. The many transportation woes involving ongoing missed connections for passengers, freight and the mail moving between the two lines eventually reached scandalous proportions.[9]

In November 1897, officials with the Grand Trunk changed the rail timetable which resulted in the Pacific Express line (another incorporated section within the rail system) arriving at Scotia Junction half an hour after the train from Parry Sound had left. The explanation given was that the change allowed the trains using the Grand Trunk (Toronto to North Bay) to make connections with other trains arriving from Western Ontario further along the line. In order to

The Albion Hotel

adjust the schedule, managing officials with the Canada Atlantic Railway rearranged their timetable to bring the evening train to Scotia Junction two hours ahead of the normal schedule. A compromise had finally been reached, thanks to the intervention of the Toronto Board of Trade and the *Toronto Globe* newspaper.[10] The new arrangement had trains leaving Toronto at 11:55 a.m. reaching Scotia Junction at 5:35 p.m., with the return trip through the junction at 9:35 a.m., arriving in Toronto at 3:00 p.m. This now meant connections were made with both morning and evening trains running on the Canada Atlantic rail lines. The final scheduling change resulted in only a slight inconvenience for the Parry Sound trains, which now left the Scotia Junction station 10 minutes earlier in the morning, arriving 10 minutes later at night. It was with a certain amount of optimism that the district newspaper was to finally conclude, "The scandalous delay at Scotia Junction is now thing of the past and now the Grand Trunk and the C.A. & P.S. Railways make sharp connections both north and south as well as east and west."[11]

That optimism, unfortunately, was to be short-lived. What was thought to be a permanent arrangement was changed abruptly a few months later by the Grand Trunk officials. The southbound morning train (North Bay to Toronto) was rescheduled through Scotia Junction one hour earlier (8:35 a.m.) and the northbound train in Toronto was held back until 3:15 p.m. Although the Parry Sound morning timetable was changed accordingly, it soon became evident that the evening train could not be delayed. As a result, passengers, freight and mail had a 24 hour wait at Scotia for Grand Trunk's morning train, a delay of much inconvenience.[12]

This went on for several months, causing some local freight to be diverted through Ottawa and Montreal, instead of Toronto and Hamilton. The situation deteriorated to the point where the Postmaster General was urged to cancel the mail contract with railways and forward it by stage if necessary. But once again, rail officials with the Grand Trunk had a timely explanation, pointing out that their rescheduling was necessary in order to connect with the eastbound CPR trains at Toronto and North Bay. It was argued that to reverse the timetable to its former schedule would inconvenience a greater number of people than those that were being served by the trains running on the Canada Atlantic rail line. In otherwords, the amount of business received at Scotia Junction was so small it wasn't worth the effort.[13] Grand Trunk officials alleged that the amount of passenger business from the Canada Atlantic rail line worked out to approximately $137 a month. Conflicting reports stated that the actual figure stood closer to $300 a month when passenger travel income was combined with freight rates, express earnings and mail contracts.[14]

Despite all efforts the timetable problem never was resolved and it continued to plague local officials and the station agent at Scotia Junction. But that was now the least of their worries. The heyday of the railroads was losing its bloom. By the 1920s the railway companies, which built communities like Scotia

After the railway lost its importance, Scotia dwindled down to a few buildings as shown by this view of the main street (c. 1920s).

The last steamer. After Scotia had become the crossroads of two great railways, docks and grain elevators were being built at Depot or Parry Harbour for big lake vessels. Wheat, flour and many kinds of merchandise were shipped over the line. However, the great days of the railroads began to wane and the railway towns like Scotia Junction dwindled in importance.

Junction, were no longer prominent in the transportation business and, by the late 1930s, they had passed on into history. However, railway tracks and railway cars continued to cover the swamp at Scotia and buildings clustered around the junction. There were engine sheds, freight sheds, section houses and even the replacement railway station, built in 1914, quite a sizable structure. A good restaurant located just at the bottom of the hill south of the station continued to do a brisk business right up until the last days. In 1920s it was still considered the best eating place between Huntsville and North Bay.[15]

Throughout the short history of the railway between Parry Sound and Ottawa, washouts and mechanical problems caused trains to make unscheduled stops along the line on a continuous basis. However, there also were stops made for entirely different reasons. It has been said that, during the night,

flickering fires dotted the hills like fireflies between Kearney and Whitney. Those fires are said to have belonged to the 'moonshiners.' There appeared to be no lack of customers, as the moonshiners' steady clientele included some of the railway crews. Railside encounters were jokingly referred to, among the railway fraternity, as 'cornfield meets.'[16] There were so many stills in the area at one point that local stores had trouble keeping enough Guillett's Lye in stock. Not only was lye used in the production of moonshine, it was also needed as well for swabbing the floors of railway stations and sleeping cars.

On a more legitimate note, the Canada Atlantic Rail line may have passed through moonshine territory, but it also carried large quantities of government regulated liquor westward, on a regular basis, from Montreal via Ottawa to Scotia Junction. Here it was reloaded onto the Grand Trunk line to the north and west. One such shipment, four full box cars of whiskey, arrived and was placed on a siding at Scotia Junction. The entire set of box cars disappeared, with only empty box cars being located on a spur line in Toronto several weeks later.[17] Just who hijacked the whiskey remains a mystery to this day.

In August of 1904, the sale of the Canada Atlantic to the Grand Trunk was agreed to in principle and J.R. Booth was elected a director of the Grand Trunk Pacific. By the end of the negotiations, Booth collected $16,000,000 for his holdings.[18] It was all over by 1923, as the Grand Trunk itself became part of Canadian National, signalling the end of one of the most glorious eras in transportation.[19]

5   Murder at Emsdale

Emsdale, first located up on the hill west of where the community is today, moved railside in 1886. But just before the settlement's relocation, its lone tavern became the site of a gruesome murder. The infamous Coleman House, at the junction of what now is known as Star Lake Road and the Old Government Road, may have been a hotel, but for all intents and purposes it resembled nothing more than an old stable built of rough hewn lumber, one storey high.[1]

It was during the final stages of railway construction through the area in 1884 and the following year, that an Irish teamster was to commit a murder on these premises. According to the oldtimers, the tavern had always had a bad reputation. "More fights occurred there than at any other hotel along the whole line of railway."[2] And there were many opportunities for brawls. At any given time there were large numbers of labourers with their teams in the area, hauling materials to the railroad gang and, after the day's work was done, they always made it a point to stop at Coleman's.

The night of the murder was no different than any other. It was a cold Wednesday in March 1885, that found Huntsville coroner, Captain Macfarlane, enroute to Emsdale, accompanied by Constable T.W. George. The purpose in making this day and a half long trip was to hold an inquest into the death of a man killed in a drunken bar-room fight at the hotel. In the evidence taken at the inquest it appeared that Michael Kelpin, sub-contractor on the Northern & Pacific Junction Railway, along with 19-year-old Thomas Kearney of Dublin, Ireland, a teamster employed by

Kelpin, and Thomas 'Gooney' Young arrived together at Coleman's Hotel in Emsdale. Having come down from Katrine the previous Monday, the trio were in a drunken state by the time they reached Emsdale.

Heading straight for the bar where a number of men were drinking, according to witnesses, 'Gooney' immediately got into an argument with one of the workers on the rail line. It all started when the labourer, James Toomy, gave Young a sideways glance that Toomy misinterpreted. Kearney interrupted the dispute between the two men, stating, that 'Gooney' was a friend of his and James Toomy was to leave him alone. Seeing that Toomy was ignoring the warning, Thomas Kearney hit him.

After being hit a second time, James Toomy decided to defend himself and soon he had the better of Kearney, pinning him to the bar-room floor. James Toomy only let his

The Maples on Star Lake Road. William Acton moved his family up from Orillia in 1896, ten years after the railway pushed through Emsdale. He built his model farm, named The Maples, close to where Emsdale was first situated. Star Lake Road was the route settlers used to get from Emsdale to Sequin Falls. The Maples exists to this day.

aggressor up on the intervention of the bar-keeper, mumbling that he didn't wish to hurt Kearney. After the man left the bar and went into the hotel's sitting room across the hall, Thomas Kearney rushed out of the hotel. Unhooking the traces of his team, he removed one of the whiffletrees. Dashing back into the bar brandishing his weapon and swearing that he would kill James Toomy, he strode around the room for some time, continuing his threats. Finally spotting his intended victim in the sitting room, Thomas Kearney surged at the man, striking Toomy on the left side of the head, above the ear.

Toomy fell into the corner and while he lay there senseless, Kearney raised the whiffletree to strike again, but was prevented from doing so by the barkeeper who shoved him out the door. In the meantime, two other men were brawling outside and Thomas Kearney, upon seeing this fight, went up to them and struck one with the whiffletree. Returning to the bar, Kearney next spotted his boss, engaged in a fight with a shoemaker named Rook. It was then that Kearney asked Kelpin if he wanted the shoemaker dead. Wrestling

the unfortunate shoemaker to the floor, Kearney turned to his employer and said, "Shall I kill him?" "Yes," said Kelpin. "Kill him dead, and then swing for it like a man."[3]

Coleman himself having just returned to his hotel, went behind the bar for his club and warned Kearney not to strike at Rook again, or he would take the club to him. Michael Kelpin pulled his revolver and threatened to shoot Coleman if he interfered. It was then that Coleman's 16-year-old daughter ran into the bar and pulled Michael Kelpin backwards on the floor. Her father told Kelpin to put away his pistol, which he did.

But in the meantime, Thomas Kearney continued beating the shoemaker over the head with the whiffletree, only stopping when the crowd interfered and wrestled the weapon away from the drunken man. It was given to Coleman who immediately hid it. Almost instinctively, Michael Keplin, Thomas Kearney and Thomas Young left Coleman's and headed south on the Muskoka Road.

James Toomy who at first appeared to have recovered from the blow to his head, began complaining of feeling sick. He went to

The Perry Township Agricultural Society was formed in 1890, later amalgamating with the neighbouring McMurrich Township. It evolved into the Emsdale Agricultural Society. Fall Fairs played an important role in community life, attracting huge crowds as this photo from the early part of the 1900s shows. After World War II, the interest waned. By the mid 1950s the Emsdale Fall Fair experienced a revival and the renewed interest continues to this day.

South Church Street in Emsdale. The main business section of town was located along this stretch of road. One of the more famous merchants was Alex Freeland. His store is located midway down the street. Called 'split raisin' Freeland, he was known to bite a raisin in half to make the weight. The Freelands were Irish and moved from southern Ontario to Emsdale in 1867, when Alex was four years old. He died in 1936, one year after Emsdale's worst fire.

his bed and that was the last time anyone saw him alive. Two 'navvies' slept in the same room as James Toomy, but seemingly did not notice anything unusual. The next morning around 9 o'oclock, Coleman asked one of them how the man was. Upon going back to the room, they discovered that James Toomy was dead.

A coroner was sent for by Coleman himself. In the meantime Thomas Kearney was captured near Utterson and taken back up to Emsdale, where he arrived in time to be present at the inquest. Dr. Francis Howland of Huntsville made the post mortem examination, stating that James Toomy suffered from an extensive fracture to the skull. A jury, assembled for the inquest, brought in the verdict that James Toomy came to his death by a blow from a whippletree, struck by one Thomas Kearney who was in the state of public intoxication at the time of the attack.[4]

Captain Macfarlane issued a warrant and sent Thomas Kearney to Barrie to stand trial. Was he found guilty? Did he go to prison, or was he hanged? His fate will never be known as court records from the time are unavailable. And while the court system dealt with Thomas Kearney, in the meantime Michael Kelpin had disappeared, never to be heard from again.

Emsdale moved railside within the year and the incident at Coleman's was never spoken of again. The hotel fell into ruin, its exact location to remain as mysterious as the disappearance of Michael Kelpin.

6 | The Highlander and the Temperance Movement

Scottish highlander Alexander Begg envisioned greatness for the newly opened wilderness almost as soon as he set foot in the area in late 1867. By happy coincidence, McMurrich Township commorated another Scotsman, John McMurrich, a fact that did not go unnoticed by Begg. As a member of the provincial government from 1867 to 1871, John McMurrich was entitled to have a township named after him. Alexander Begg took this as a sign of divine providence. What an ideal spot for a Temperance colony! Since Begg was a member of the Temperance Society, an organization which called for total abstinence from intoxicants, the township's virtual isolation in the midst of a vast unbroken forest, almost guaranteed compliance from the settlers. Or so Alexander Begg thought.[1]

Born in 1825, Begg emigrated to Canada West (the name used to identify what is now Ontario before Confederation) as a young man, during the height of the potato famine which ravaged both Ireland and Scotland. And by the time Begg had reached middle age, his adopted country had become a struggling new nation. It was a truly exciting time and the diminutive Scotsman was ready for it, travelling back and forth to Kingston on a regular basis, firming up his plans for the new Temperance colony which was to include a mill site.

Begg was to sideline his plans temporarily and join a survey crew while the federal government prepared for the governance transfer of the North West Territories from the Hudson's Bay Company to Canada, and for the Red River area as well. It was in 1869 that Prime Minister Sir John A. MacDonald,

appointed William McDougall as lieutenant governor of this new territory and Begg signed up as secretary and historian with McDougall.[2] However, Louis Riel's Red River Insurrection resisted the government's attempt to arbitrarily incorporate the colony. The survey crew sent to Red River was stopped in its tracks by Riel's National Committee, fearful of the impending influx of aggressive Anglo-Protestant immigrants from Ontario and beyond.[3] With McDougall prevented from entering the Red River settlement, one month later he would return east with both his son who had served as French interpreter and Alexander Begg. It was not until July 15, 1870, that the transfer of territories was completed and, in the same year, following the defeat of the Metis under Riel, Sir John A. MacDonald created the small province of Manitoba, with Winnipeg as its central focus.

Invigorated by his travels and experiences out west, Begg returned to McMurrich Township to begin his search for a mill site in earnest. Having reached the northeast shore of Doe Lake, one day while walking along a portage trail accompanied by an unnamed friend, he suddenly stopped and stood silent on the path. Hearing the roar of water in the distance, Begg asked, "What now, where are the falls?" His friend turned to reply, "Oh, that's a fall to the southwest of us, just where this river feeds the lake." "The very thing," continued Begg. "How can we get there?" "Well," said the friend, "I have been across the water and up the river, but I don't believe anything but an Indian or an animal used to these woods, could find them by a land

Impressive is the only word to use in describing the *Nipissing*—a 52 tonne sidewheeler that plied the waters of Muskoka. Travellers heading into the newly opened territory that included the region now known as Almaguin, would take the *Nipissing* as far as Rosseau, before heading up the Rosseau-Nipissing Colonization Road. Added to the fleet in 1871, the *Nipissing* was lost to fire in 1885 while moored at Port Cockburn on Lake Joseph.

route."[4] Not to be put off, Alexander Begg continued his quest and was rewarded for his efforts. Situating himself at a spot where he could view the thirty foot channel of deep water roaring over a precipice, 12 to 14 yards in height, he was thoroughly enchanted with the place. What a fortune he would make of such water power!

The Temperance Society, based in Kingston during the 1870s, was federally supported and Begg set about to obtain a commission from them. He was determined that his mill site would be located in McMurrich Township and he concluded that the large number of settlers, who were temperance supporters at the time, would make the building of a mill an extremely profitable speculation considering the region's vast spruce, balsam, hemlock and soft wood forests. Begg knew he had found better than what he was looking for, or expected. His temperance colony, Beggsboro, became the township's first settlement.

However, by the mid 1870s, very little news about the newly opened territory had actually reached the outside world. The only link with Alexander Begg's neighbourhood located deep in the wilds was the 'Missionary Road' built to connect the Nipissing Colonization Road with Doe Lake.[5] At first settlers were unable to cross into the new territory in their low, sled-shaped 'sloops' drawn by oxen. Travelling by wagon train remained prohibitive until road conditions improved in 1878. Hence, the most common route, taken by intrepid travellers determined to make their way north, was by train to the last whistle stop on the line at Severn Bridge in north Orillia Township. From here a stagecoach to Gravenhurst would connect the traveller with the steamer *Nipissing*. Having traversed the full length of lakes Muskoka and Rosseau, the steamer would make a stop at the village of Rosseau where the passengers would disembark.

The *Nipissing,* an impressive sidewheeler of 52 tonnes, carried both freight and passengers. One of several paddlewheel boats to ply the waters of Muskoka, the *Nipissing* was added to the fleet in 1871. She had main, upper and hurricane decks, and was said to serve exceptionally good meals. A dollar went a long way those days and, at a hotel for instance, it was possible to get three meals and a bed for that dollar.[6] Dinner on board the *Nipissing* was much the same fare as served at a good frontier hotel. A typical meal would consist of soup, roast beef, roast pork, steamed pudding, apple pie, tea or good stout ale. Unfortunately, the sidewheeler mysteriously burned down to the water line one night while moored at the Port Cockburn dock on Lake Joseph.[7]

For many onboard the *Nipissing*, it would be the last good meal for some time. Once the settlers left the steamer at Rosseau, they then began the long arduous journey on foot, up the Nipissing Road to Sequin Falls and from there to continue eastwards on the Missionary Road to Beggsboro. To access any place further east there was another trail called the Perry and Montieth Road, cutting through to Perry Township. This trail did not begin to resemble anything like an actual road until 1879 when the last two and a half miles were completed.[8] Fortunately, by 1874 a stagecoach road, connecting the Muskoka communities of Gravenhurst, Bracebridge, Utterson and Huntsville to Emsdale, was in full operation. A section of this road, going north from Bracebridge and called the Stisted Road, dead-ended at the northern boundary of McMurrich Township supposedly "at the home of a certain long suffering pioneer called Job."[9]

As more and more roads opened up and the influx of settlers began, the dangers and adventures experienced in just getting to the township, compounded by the incredible isolation and hard work required once they did arrive, found many of the newcomers seeking comfort in self indulgence. Namely whiskey.

Most settlers 'liked to take a drink,' and did not see anything wrong with it. For a while, in the late 1880s, there appeared to be a sufficient number of Temperance supporters among the new arrivals to cause a Good Templar's Lodge and Literary Society to spring up in nearby Sprucedale. Local Temperance supporters heralded the founder of the local movement, a Mr. Dawson, and were convinced that if the community's young people could be steered away from the whiskey mill, that was an accomplishment in itself.[10]

Good fortune was to come to the Lodge in Sprucedale, for on the evening of April 12, 1889, the neighbouring municipality's Temperance organizer, Duncan Marshall of Perry Township, paid an official visit and gave a moving Temperance lecture in the Methodist Church to a large and very attentive audience. Marshall did not follow the usual line of Temperance lectures, bewailing the tribulations of the drunkard and his suffering family. Temperance supporters were well aware of the demoralizing influence of the liquor trade, a fact that couldn't be stated strongly enough in all its harrowing details. However, the Perry Township Good Templar directed the thoughts of his audience to the practical duty of the hour, the political clout of the Temperance Society.

According to Duncan Marshall, one undisputed fact sustaining them was that the Prohibition vote was clean, true and represented the moral sentiment of the nation. Why, he informed them, a majority of nearly 14,000 people voted in favour of Prohibition only just recently! To back up their vote, Temperance members were urged to start up petitions in local churches and other societies, and then present them to their municipal representatives. Duncan Marshall assured the audience, that such action clearly would show that any party or politician seeking the 'suffrages' of the people, must demonstrate a willingness to obey their expressed wishes. The lecture attracted nine new members, and Duncan Marshall conducted the initiation ceremonies of the Lodge.[11] The total membership now stood at thirty.

However, local anti-Prohibitionists in the area, began gathering strength by using the failure of other Temperance schemes in the province to their advantage. Eventually they were able to turn enough residents of the township against Alexander Begg that his Temperance dream turned into mere speculation. The movement collapsed, leaving Alexander Begg with only himself to set up as an example to incoming settlers and to convince them to take up residence in his Temperance colony.

Unfortunately for Begg, they did not, and the colony's founder was never to make Beggsboro his home. Out of his 11 children, four sons and one daughter became prominent New York City lawyers. His son William, one of those sons, did hold on to land claims in McMurrich Township, but Alexander Begg moved on with his wife Emily to New York, severing all ties.[12] It is known that Alexander Begg died in New York in 1903 at the age of 79, but was buried in the family plot in St. Andrew's Cemetery in Orillia. Throughout his very public life he remained a very wealthy if not, at the end, a very disappointed man.[13]

7 | David Francis Burk

What was it about this new unknown territory that motivated so many to leave the familiarity of established towns and cities of southern Ontario? Even when it became apparent that the free grants were to be routinely suspended by the government, unannounced and without explanation, it did little to stop the flow of people. Settlers came along and took up vacant lands, paying 70 cents per acre for them in cash, or $1 on time.[1] The prospects of wealth and the chance to create something of one's very own in the wilderness provided a powerful incentive.

Some, of course, viewed the north as a holiday destination, gathering small groups of neighbours and friends together during the summertime for the excursion. Travel to the backwoods, often reserved for the men folk, usually took place later in the season to avoid grueling heat and intolerable black flies, but not too late. Although cold nights would have provided better opportunities for fishing and hunting, they definitely were unsuitable for camping.

In southern Ontario, for the idle rich and the adventurous of the times, the actual destination didn't matter. It could be to the backwoods, or then again to the seaside. Or better yet, fashionable places in Europe where they could take their wives. Once the travellers were off, the rest of the household was then left to settle in and eagerly await for their return. Afterwards, many an hour was spent in conversation over the latest adventure. The best stories were about those so-called backwoods. Often listeners were so captivated by what they heard, they sometimes jumped at the chance for similar adventures themselves.

Others took the stories on an even more serious note and made their trips—one way.

One such person who bought a one way ticket was David Francis Burk of Oshawa. His father, David Burk Sr., who was not only the reeve of Oshawa that year but a successful area farmer as well, had taken a trip north in late August of 1865. Apparently leaving his farming operation to hired hands and family members, he travelled to the beautiful inland lakes and rivers of the Muskokas with three companions: Samuel Luke, an English newspaperman with the *Oshawa Vindicator*, John Edwin Chandler Farewell, a barrister with the Oshawa firm of Farewell and McGee, and a news correspondent with the *Toronto Globe*. And what a trip it was to be! The starting point for the excursion began on August 23, 1865 at Lake Simcoe, taking the foursome up the north branch of the Muskoka River to Vernon Lake and then crossing over to the head waters of the Trent River.

The travellers left Oshawa on the Wednesday night, the first leg to take them to the Severn River. Their two boats and their luggage were apparently transported by team to Beaverton. By the end of September, Burk Sr. and his friends had reached Bracebridge. It certainly had been no easy task. A diary kept by the news correspondent, who was never to be identified by name, recorded the activity the day before the group made it to the settlement. The very first excerpt would appear in the October 4, 1865 edition of the *Toronto Globe*. Of course, Burk's son Frank found it even more fun to read because he had been privy to the inside story told by his father. David Sr., it appears, 'filled in all the blanks', and according to him the news correspondent had apparently left out the best parts!

It appears that the foursome took on an Indian guide by the name of Charles Jacobs at Rama and, though heavily provisioned, caught many of their meals themselves during the expedition.[2]

"Tuesday, 28th—Got the boats over the half-mile portage before breakfast, so that on breaking camp all hands moved on. A pull of a mile across the northern leg of the lake brought us to the two-mile portage into Muskoka Bay. Passing the boats and luggage over this rough and swampy portage, occupied the greater part of the day. The Indian, our guide informed us, call it two miles, while the white people call it three. The whole party came to the unanimous conclusion, that the white men were right, and that the Indian measurement must have been made on snow shoes, or in other light travelling trim. In the evening, crossed the Muskoka Bay, a distance of a mile and a half, to a point where the Muskoka (colonization) Road touches it, and camped for the night. "Wednesday, 29th—Breakfasted early, and started up the bay. A favourable breeze springing up, one of the boats took to sails, while the other took it easy with the oars, and passing through the eastern portion of the lake, reached the first fall on the north branch of the Muskoka River, a distance of 15 miles before noon...."[3]

It was here at a Bracebridge hotel, that Burk Sr. and his friends were to met up with a gentleman who was referred to as Mr. Oliver. He was the government agent in charge of the Muskoka (colonization) Road. During their conversation, the Oshawa men gathered a great deal of information from Oliver on the settlement, and the new road going north.

Oliver had some 58 men employed along different sections of this road, most of them working at that time on the northern portion that would one day connect with the Parry Sound (colonization) Road.

Later back at camp, while members of the Burk party were enjoying dinner with their new acquaintances, a deer wandered towards them. Somehow, it managed to escape a shot from one of the Burk party's guns, by boldly coming right into the camp. The newcomers were informed by the locals that it was a tame deer belonging to the local postmaster, Alex Bailey. Burk Sr., Luke, Farewell and the newspaper correspondent sat back and marvelled how the deer then took bread and salt from their hands.

The deer was not the only chance encounter the men would experience. A tame gull which lit on the river within gunshot, would possibly have fared badly as well if Burk's party hadn't been cautioned. The group eventually reached the conclusion that "it would not do to shoot at any living thing in this neighbourhood, lest it might be somebody's pet."[4]

Travelling, for necessity' sake or pleasure, was something with which the Burks were all too familiar. Frank's great, great-grandfather Francis Burk, had immigrated as a child from Ireland to America in 1725. Almost seventy years later, his son John Burk, enticed by land grants, and wishing to take shelter under British rule, uprooted his entire family from their home near the north branch of the Susquehanna River in upper New York State and moved to Upper Canada.[5] John Burk became one of the first United Empire Loyalist settlers to take up residence in Darlington Township (east of York) in October of 1794. After receiving his own land grant of four hundred acres in 1798 alongside the swift flowing Barber (Bowmanville) Creek, he proceeded over time to acquire over one thousand acres of land on which he built the first grist mill and first saw mill. By the 1820s he had added a store and an inn and was now a man of prominence.

His great, grandson, Frank Burk was just a teenager when his father went off to the Muskokas. Nine years later in 1874, now a young man in his 20s, Frank ventured even further north than his father had. So enchanted by what he saw, he ended up clearing two acres of land just below the junction of the south branch of the Magnetawan River, at the point where it veered off to the west. Was it the stories his father told about his holiday north that prompted Frank to strike it out into the newly opened territory? Or was he simply following in John Burk's footsteps? It is likely that Burk Sr.'s excursion must have stuck a cord in Frank's mind. The travelling done by his father through new and interesting countryside, made real through stories, and his father's talk of the colonization roads, which were pushing even further north, likely caught the young man's imagination.

In 1876, Frank Burk returned to his land claim on the Magnetawan River with his wife Olive. Constructing a log shanty by the falls, he became the first white settler to take up permanent residence in the area.[6] Frank later replaced his shanty with a large square cut log house, which he promptly christened the Burk House. It was not only a home, but a hotel, post office, general store and church for the new settlement.

John Burk eventually left the Bowmanville area and returned to the United States in 1818, leaving his family and descendants to inherit the massive Burk property, which later became Darlington Provincial Park and the site for the Darlington Generating Station.[7] As for his great grandson, Frank Burk, he was to die on June 13, 1901, in the community he founded and where he was buried. His only son Walter, passed away the following year. Frank's widow Olive, along with their two daughters, Mabel and Ida, are reported to have moved out of Ontario to Zion City, Illinois. Unfortunately, their final resting place has never been determined, as Zion City cemetery records of the time no longer exist. Also there are no records left to verify that the widow Burk and her daughter actually left the province after her husband's death.

In honour of its first settler, the community adopted Frank Burk's name as its own when it incorporated in 1890. Unfortunately, the Burk House, along with the main business section of the village, burnt to the ground eighteen years later in the fire of 1908.

8 | Enroute to Burk's Falls!

By 1883, less than ten years after David Francis Burk staked his claim at the foot of the falls on the Magnetawan River, the new territory had blossomed with tiny settlements. Along the twenty-eight mile stretch from Huntsville to Burk's Falls, the countryside was dotted with stump and stone-dotted clearings, settlers' shanties, log huts and the ever-recurring wriggling lines of snake fences. Most of the dwellings sprinkled here and there, along with the occasional little church, were built of plain unpainted pine, very quaint, and sometimes very unusual. When families needed more space—they simply added on a lean-to at the side of the house, and there was the new bedroom or kitchen![1]

For those settlers who chose Burk's Falls as their site for staking land claims, it seemed like only yesterday when Katrine had been the end of the road for them. In 1877 this settlement had been the furthest point north of Huntsville where one could find a post office and general store. At that time, in order to push on to Burk's Falls, new settlers had to cross the Magnetawan River outlet at Doe Bay on a make-shift bridge of flattened timber. By the following year the few, more or less permanent residents, decided to replace the temporary structure and built a real bridge to span the river, a step that encouraged more northerly expansion. Finally, in 1879, permanent wooden bridges were built by the provincial government at both Katrine and Burk's Falls.[2]

The stagecoach ride from Huntsville to Burk's Falls was anything but smooth. In one of her many diaries, English artist and Salvationist (as Salvation Army members were called at the time), Ada Florence Kinton decided to document her one and only trip there that was taken in the spring of 1883. "Riding since 7:30 in the morning in the stage in the midst of six men, including the driver, Mack, and four bronzed, happy-tempered laborers or settlers, jolting and swaying up and down hill and dale, over stones unnumbered, through mud and mire, over corduroy bridges, and swamps waving with beaver grass, and then though the deep bush."[3] This run north from Huntsville sometimes cut through clearings that gave the passengers a glimpse of long vistas of undulating hills and swift flowing water before plunging back into a densely walled-in stretch of mighty pines. From time to time there would be a number of blackened and charred spaces where fires ravaged the forest—the tell-tale signature of numerous journeyman lumbermen which plagued the region.

One of the first communities north of Huntsville was Melissa, followed by several more little villages including Novar and Cyprus. Most consisted of a half dozen houses, a general store, a church, sometimes a school house and a roadside inn. Primitive in their appearance, all the buildings were constructed of wood. The only brick-clad home at the time was located in Huntsville. It belonged to its first reeve, Louis E. Kinton.

Before the railway came, the first actual designated stagecoach stop north of Huntsville was Cyprus, situated in Perry Township. Here passengers could get the first decent dinner in what passed for a hotel.[4] Called the Traveller's Rest, it was owned and operated by Dunk Woodrow. Despite the ambitious label of

Ontario Street, Burk's Falls. A view looking south. Dirt roads and wooden sidewalks ruled the day, making pedestrian traffic a challenge, especially when going uphill!

hotel, it was little more than a shanty with the typical bare walls and low, slanting ceilings.[5]

Cyprus, like Novar to the south of it, was a depot for a variety of supplies coming north from Bracebridge for distribution in the new territory. Since the teamsters needed accommodation while the loads were being transferred from one wagon to another, Woodrow expanded his original roadside inn with a lean-to in order to accommodate the men. Sensing that he was onto a good thing, he eventually dressed the place up a bit with bright prints to decorate the sitting room walls and called the place a hotel.[6] Strips of homemade carpet covered the pine board floors and customers sat on rough wooden chairs. One thing could be said for Woodrow, his place was clean and wholesome with a plentiful supply of food set out on spotless tablecloths. The menu consisted of the usual meal offered in the backwoods stop overs, with small variations. Eggs and bacon, mashed potatoes, tea, two or three kinds of cookies, biscuits, homemade bread and, of course, gooseberry pie.[7]

Cyprus made the most of its depot status. A post office was opened, as was a small general store to carry some of the goods brought in from Bracebridge for local consumption.[8] A modest little church, St. Margaret's Anglican, was filled with about twenty chairs plus a reading desk, covered with red cotton.[9] The traditional little pointed windows that lined the outside walls, allowed the congregation a glimpse of scenery—a diversion from the steady view of altar pieces.[10]

Once rested, the traveller would resume the trip to Burk's Falls. The road north of Cyprus ran through picturesque countryside that became especially prominent during a cloudy day. Silhouetted against the grey skies were the tall, magestic trees and sometimes, as Ada Kinton described it, "long glimmering streaks of hazy grey and yellow in the skies above would make an uneven reflection on the dark, wide waters of a nearby pine-girdled lake."[11] However, it did little to detract from the realities of how difficult the journey really was. Once out among the beaver grass and flooded land, passengers on the stagecoach often ended up on foot. Frequently mishaps occurred. Sometimes a horse would falter and fall in the water. This would delay the stage for sometime and once the journey resumed, there would always be something to contend with ahead, possibly heavy going through thick mud or terrain so uneven that passengers frequently found themselves clutching the stagecoach walls with both hands to avoid being flung out among the rocks. But by sundown, Burk's Falls was within view.[12]

Visitors that subjected themselves to the tortures of the road between Huntsville and Burk's Falls eventually were rewarded with a view of the Magnetawan River, its rapids and the falls themselves. According to Ada Kinton, there were few things so exhilarating as a stroll along the banks of the boiling falls itself. In her dairies, she described it as "A marvellous sight—in its boiling, broken tumbling tumult of fall and swirling rapids, in its uneven channel, dashing foaming, frothing over sunken and jagged rocks, piling up its creamy heaps of amber foam, tossing showers of snowy spray, bubbling and seething, dancing a mad, frantic waltz in dazzling circles, roaring, raving, hissing, thundering, booming, rushing violently headlong downwards, shattering its troubled mass into quivering fountains, and fretting from side to side and to and fro between its rocky margin, till all the inky current is marbled over with yellow bubbling froth and then hurrying wildly, deafeningly, away down in the coiling bed of the Magnetawan River a long, narrow quiet steady stream."[13]

Not bad for a fall that only extended 20 feet.

When James Sharpe first arrived to Burk's Falls in the late 1870s, the settlement was little more than a clearing in the bush. The number of families actually living in the community could be counted on one hand, with about as many in the surrounding area.

David Francis Burk, or Frank as he was called, was the original homesteader to stake his claim in the area. And one of the first things he did when more settlers began to trickle into the area, was oversee the extension of the Muskoka (colonization) Road, northward from Burk's Falls into Strong Township.[1] Burk strongly believed that a good network of roads would help retain permanent residents.[2] Certainly the settlement had potential for growth, with its principal feature being the Magnetewan River and the 'pretty' falls so familiar to scene-loving tourists. James Sharpe was one of those incoming settlers, but before even making the final move north to Burk's Falls from Chaffey Township in Muskoka District, Sharpe threw himself into helping Burk develop the new community. Before long, favourable reports of the Armour Road extension to the north-east corner of Pickerel Lake, being built under Sharpe's supervision, began reaching government road agents. However, it wasn't enough to convince the man to make his stay in the community a permanent one. When John Scarlett came to Burk's Falls with his mercantile business plans, that's when James Sharpe made up his mind. He knew Scarlett from his days in the Huntsville area and considered him a good businessman.

Confident that the tranquil beauty of the spot would attract great numbers of new residents, James Sharpe set about creating a home for himself and his family. Unfortunately, the peacefulness that he so enjoyed soon was interrupted. It was six o'clock in the morning, the beginning of a new day and a new week. September 29, 1885 would be a day long remembered by James Sharpe. A severe thunderstorm had been gathering momentum during the night and, at the break of dawn, the village was shaken by what appeared to be a dynamite explosion. Because of the early hour, only a few residents, including Sharpe, were dressed for the day. Out they rushed onto the main street to determine the source of the unexpected sound.

It soon became apparent that the cause of the dreadful noise had been a tremendous bolt of lightening striking the building which housed both the business and residence of one Robert H. Menzies. Onlookers, along with Sharpe, began tracing the path of the current which appeared to have travelled down the stove pipe. When it reached the main floor stove, located above the cellar, to everyone's amazement, the current for some unexplained reason, separated here. Passing through the floor in two places at both the front and the rear of the stove, the lightning strike had left in its wake two gaping holes, each about 1 1/2 inches in diameter. Amazingly the stove was not broken and the stove pipes remained in position. It was one heck of a way to clean out the stove pipes, as one onlooker pointed out, for upon examining them, it was discovered that the soot had been completely removed.[3]

Menzies and a small group then ventured into the cellar, to check for any other damage. They were to find a number of household articles thrown around and some papers set on fire inside a tin dish! What was so astonishing about the whole thing, was that this dish was several feet away from the point where the lightening had finally entered the ground! The only other casualty had been the kitchen cook stove. Located in another part of the house, the tremendous jolt had caused it to fall apart. Everyone agreed, it was a miracle that Menzies and his family had escaped unharmed, despite the severe shock they received.

After interest in the calamity of that day finally died down, Sharpe turned his attentions back to his partnership with John Scarlett. However, in the long run despite all good intentions, the mercantile business venture didn't hold much interest for either partner, and the decision was made to hire a local man by the name of William Copeland to manage Scarlett's general store.[4]

Earlier predictions of growth proved to be right on course and Burk's Falls continued to expand. However, it wasn't until the advent of the railway in 1885 that any real boom occurred. At this point, Sharpe decided to go into the hotel business. Offering more accommodation certainly would attract more potential residents to the community. And so he began building the Clifton House on the main street of Burk's Falls, completing it in 1887, exactly two years after the railway pushed through.

Although the Burk House enjoyed a commanding view of the river and falls, Sharpe's fancy new hotel quickly became a popular stop for the influx of travellers. Despite his success, James Sharpe sold the Clifton House to Fred Brasher in 1889. Still riding high on its popularity, by 1892, the Clifton House had been enlarged by the new owner to include rooms for 60 guests and stabling for ten teams of horses. And, like the Burk House, it too ran a bus service to the train station and docks to accommodate hotel guests.[5]

It was also in 1889 that Sharpe finally disposed of his interests in the general store. With his partner Scarlett long gone to Nipissing, there was no point in holding on to the business. Besides, he had a ready buyer for the place, Louis E. Kinton. Sharpe made the wise calculation that this man would jump at the chance of getting out of politics. After having enjoyed three years of being the first reeve of Huntsville and by acclamation no less, Kinton was still smarting over the loss of his seat that same year to Dr. Francis Howland. His successor had become very popular with the Huntsville residents since taking up permanent residence back in 1875. As Kinton saw it, Dr. Howland would never have settled in the village in the first place, if it hadn't been for the government's offer of that $1,000 bonus to attract physicians to the north.[6]

James Sharpe, now rid of business responsibilities for the time being, had the opportunity to turn his attention to his fight for compulsory free education for the community's children. Observers could see that he was one of the few men of the time who understood that education was not something to be endured, but something that was to be fostered and encouraged in a growing country. In order to exert some influence on educational decision making, Sharpe decided to sit as a member of the local school board.[7] The education system at the time was a far cry from what it is today. Each community had its own school board comprised of its more prominent citizens and it appears that they voted each other on to that board.

When the day came that the settlement was to become a bonafide municipality, Sharpe decided to run for reeve. According to election results printed in the *Burk's Falls Arrow* of May 2, 1890, James Sharpe garnered 52 votes, with R. H Menzies receiving 35. Those running for council and successful in their bid were: Moses Robinson, 63; J. C.

Mitchell, 62; Captain William Kennedy, 51 and Louis M Smith, 47. Again, they were all close associates of Sharpe's. The losers were John D. Reid, 31 votes and Obadian Chambers with just 12 votes. The clerk was Ed Bazett, who also happened to be a land surveyor. In 1890 the Village of Burk's Falls was incorporated. During those early years of the 1890s, the visionary James Sharpe also entered provincial politics and became the Liberal MPP representing the District of Parry Sound from 1891 to 1894.

Working endlessly for the community that he so loved and wanted to prosper, Sharpe once again broadened his enterprise to include the banking business and the railway on the list of his interests. With the original bank in Burk's Falls being a branch of the Mathews Bank, Sharpe reasoned, why not have a locally controlled bank. Unfortunately, no information exists today on the Mathews Bank, its origins or location of a home office. For a brief period, it was taken over by Clay, Sharpe and Co., in which he had a partial interest. However, this turned into a very short-lived business venture and the bank was quickly sold off to the Sovereign Bank. Again, no historical data exists today on the Sovereign Bank. In 1908, there was another takeover, this time by the Royal Bank of Canada, which has remained as the primary financial institution in the village to this day.[8]

At the turn of the century, James Sharpe was instrumental in obtaining the rights to the spur line which ran right into Burk's Falls to the Knight Bros. Factory from the railway station. Operated by the Magnetawan River Railway Company with Sharpe as president meant that he had the privileges of a free travel pass. His daughter, Florence M. Sharpe, used her father's railway pass one day to arrange an outing, knowing that the fastest and most convenient way to meet her friends would be by using the spur line. As she boarded the train, and showed the pass to the conductor, he looked at the young woman straight in the eye and teasingly remarked, "Why, Mr. Sharpe, how you have changed lately."[9]

Embarrassed, Florence pleaded with the conductor not to tell her father she had taken it, and would the conductor please keep this episode to himself. He did. From that day forward, Florence became a regular spur line rider with father apparently turning a blind eye to the collusion.[10]

But despite his love of children, James Sharpe was anything but an easy-going, carefree man. He was said to demand much of those whom he helped and even more of himself. In his obituary, which ran in the *Burk's Falls Arrow*, November 13, 1935, James Sharpe was described as "belonging to the race of rugged pioneers, who, equipped only with health and strength and indomitable courage, overcame the grim hardships, struggled on successfully and laid securely the foundation from which have sprung the comfort, beauty and the orderly life of this fair province. He was a man of singular qualities, deeply conscientious and trustworthy in all his dealings."

Today, all that remains in the community of the Sharpe legacy is the large family home on High Street, overlooking the banks of the Magnetawan River.

10 | Trouble at the Burk's Falls Beacon!

In the fall of 1898, the villagers of Burk's Falls found themselves embroiled in the excitement over the sensational arrest of the publishers of one of the two local newspapers. The charges of criminal libel were brought against both George Ewart and Kenneth D. McLean of the weekly *Burk's Falls Beacon*. The cause of their trouble?—their editorial comment over a High Court judge's dismissal of charges against a local ruffian. "It was a miscarriage of justice!" cried the *Beacon*![1]

The lad in question was eleven year old George Bibby, who, having been caught inside the residence of Mr. Walter Sharpe, was arrested and given a speedy preliminary trial before Justices of the Peace, James Sharpe and Frank Burk. Deciding that there was sufficient evidence against Bibby, they had him bound over for trial at the High Court in Parry Sound. In the local magistrate's haste for a speedy trial, the Burk's Falls boy wound up before Parry Sound Judge McCurry without legal representation or either parent present in court. The judge adjourned the case until at least Bibby's father could be located. By the time George Bibby appeared before him the second time, Judge McCurry was of the opinion that there was no evidence against the accused—not even evidence to show that the lad had been in the Sharpe home in the first place! The witness depositions provided no information whatsoever that any crime had been committed by the youth and having no choice but to dismiss the charge, the judge stated that there would be no justice served in finding guilt in a boy so young.

Without investigating why the charges were dropped, the *Beacon* editorial of September 9, 1898 was printed with its only evidence being supplied by Burk's Falls magistrate, James Sharpe. At the preliminary hearing Bibby had been described as a pest and a nuisance by Sharpe. The editorial was an all out attack on the presiding judge as the following editorial reveals:

> "Young George Bibby, the 12 or 13 year old thief and housebreaker, returned to town on Tuesday from Parry Sound, whither he had been committed a short time ago on a charge of housebreaking with intent to steal. How this juvenile freebooter regained his liberty is not quite understood by the monarchs of the law here, but surely there must have been a woeful dispensation of justice in the disposal of his case at Parry Sound.
>
> It is an open secret that Judge Mahaffy, of Bracebridge, has become a proverbial "terror to evil doers" by the severity of his sentences to criminals of all descriptions, and it looks as if Judge McCurry, who has just been elevated to a similar jurisdiction at Parry Sound, is desirous of gaining notoriety as a more lenient dispenser of justice.
>
> Be this as it may, and with all due respect to the two gentlemen named, the evidence adduced at Bibby's trial here before Justices Sharpe and Burk called, in our humble opinion, for a term of one or more years in some house or school of correction. Had young Bibby been the pest and nuisance in the same community which Judge McCurry honors by residing in, the chances are that the culprit would have got two or three years incarceration.

As the matter now stands other juvenile offenders, companions of the young scamp named, will see an easy egress to liberty after an arrest and imprisonment that has only the merit of making them notorious, and as a result sneak thieving and housebreaking will in all likelihood be carried on with impunity in our community."[2]

Judge McCurry, finding the article to be far removed from the truth, as well as a personal attack on his character and good name, filed a complaint before Justice of the Peace, Joseph Farrer, charging the publishers of the paper, Messrs. Ewart and McLean, with criminal libel.

To the delight of the residents of Burk's Falls, who were now completely caught up in the scandalous affair, Constable Hanna from Parry Sound was sent to Burk's Falls the following week with a warrant for the arrest of the two men. Returning by train with his prisoners that same evening, he lodged them in the district jail for the night. N.A Ray, representing the two men, dutifully entered a plea of not guilty the following morning. District Crown Attorney, W.L. Haight, appeared for Judge McCurry.

The first witness to be called was Judge McCurry himself. In the evidence given on the stand, he maintained that the information provided him in the case, was not against George Bibby, or anyone else for that matter. "The first time the accused was produced before me on August 30, in the absence of any parent or guardian or representative, I declined to accept any plea on account of his extreme youth, and an adjournment was made," said Judge McCurry. "When I asked why his father was not present, the boy said his father intended being present, but he was told by the magistrate it was not necessary. He denied any criminal intention in entering Mr. Sharpe's residence...and there was no previous criminal record against the boy."[3]

Judge McCurry told the court that by the time George Bibby's second appearance rolled around on September 3, he had made the decision to dismiss the charge. The judge maintained that there was no real evidence in the case, only a letter addressed to the crown attorney from the Burk's Falls magistrate, James Sharpe. The recommendation made in the correspondence?—a long term of imprisonment in jail or reformatory for the boy.

John D. Reid, the publisher of the *Burk's Falls Arrow* also testified, but his only evidence was that he personally knew the publishers and had picked up a copy of the September 9 *Beacon* from Kenneth McLean himself. Since George Ewart refused to take the stand, declaring the whole preliminary a waste of time, it was left up to Kenneth McLean to speak for both of them. The *Burk's Falls Beacon* editorial of September 9, testified McLean, was simply expressing general opinion. The column had been written in the interests of the community and he did not think any more about the column until his arrest.

McLean maintained there had been a miscarriage of justice, that was for certain, but it was nothing personal against judge. As one of the publishers of the *Beacon*, he had been present at the preliminary trial in Burk's Falls. What he heard as evidence most definitely supported a finding of guilt. His only explanation for the turn of events was that all the information presented had apparently not been taken down as evidence. Since it now appeared that the outcome was not the fault of the judge, the law must be at fault. After all, he himself had heard what magistrate James Sharpe had to say about Bibby and that, since the magistrate was not satisfied with the boy's dismissal, the editorial was only expressing the views of Mr. Sharpe. Kenneth McLean concluded his testimony that, if it had not been for Mr. Sharpe's stellar character and position in the community, he certainly would have thought twice about making some of the statements contained in the editorial. Finding sufficient evidence against both George Ewart and Kenneth D. McLean, the Justice of the Peace had the matter bound over for trial. Bail was denied.

As things were to turn out, the *Burk's Falls Beacon* was to be in business for another day as Ewart and McLean weathered the storm, finally clearing up matters by way of an apology to Judge McCurry.[4] Kenneth McLean eventually went to work for the *Beacon's* competition, the *Arrow.* And as for George Bibby?—well, one suspects he may have continued his shenanigans for a time, much to the ire of James Sharpe, but such happenings never made it to print again!

11 | The Great Pine Log Mystery

On July 10, 1973, during the excavation of the Burk's Falls Hotel Central parking lot, Fred Borgford of Gap Construction struck a solid object with his backhoe. Taking a closer look, Borgford found the obstacle—a huge pine pier (post) bigger than anything he'd ever seen before, measuring four feet across, and quite possibly standing 12 feet in height.

It had been cut with a broad axe, making it not only very big piece of pine, but a very old one at that. Borgford's curiosity was aroused when on examining the pier, he discovered a small round cavity carved into one end. Inside the cavity, he found an old and, what appeared to be a very rare, square green gin bottle hidden from view.

The digging beside the old hotel was for the installation of a new sewer system. During the course of the day, an elderly woman came along and remarked to Fred that she could remember hearing of an old barn that stood on the excavation site. She believed that what the workman had discovered was one of the piers for the foundation. Upon hearing about the discovery, the then editor of the *Almaguin News*, Jim Kirk-White decided the find was worth a story. He began running down a number of possible leads, however, it looked as if the origins of the massive pine post (at least that is what it looked like to him) was going to remain a mystery when he ran into a series of dead ends.

The first person he talked to was Stan Purdie, a long time employee of Hotel Central. Purdie could not recall ever hearing of any building being on the site. The barber also turned out to be of no particular help. Old Jack Wilson, who had been a resident Burk's

Falls since 1928, couldn't remember any of his customers ever mentioning anything about a building at that particular location. Kirk-White then turned to another Burk's Falls old-timer, Aubrey 'Was' West. Old 'Was' was the son of the late Joseph and Elizabeth West of Bracebridge. Born on December 5, 1895, 'Was' moved with his parents to Burk's Falls at the turn of the century and was one individual who could recollect all the way back to the days of the big fire of 1908. According to 'Was', the fire razed the whole street. Well, that was a well known fact. Unfortunately, the only other bit of news he could offer was that before the fire, the old Clifton House stood where the Hotel Central was now. Another resident, Bob Mitchell, hadn't heard of any building being there either, but swore that it was his grandfather who had been the one to put the gin bottle in the hole in the log.

By now Jim Kirk-White was beginning to feel as if he was the only one interested in determining the original use of the pine log. Everybody else was more interested in the old gin bottle. No matter who he'd talked to, they all wanted to claim credit for it. Exasperated, Kirk-White turned to the newspaper's files and, scouring old photographs taken immediately before and after the fire, located a building that he felt may have needed such a large pine log. It was a barn like structure, with a chimney and windows and stood on Ontario Street between 1885 and 1904.

One of the biggest drawbacks facing the editor was the fact that all of the earliest issues of the village's first weekly newspaper, the *Burk's Falls Arrow*, had been destroyed. Undaunted, Kirk-White turned to the *Arrow's*

A log shanty on the Rousseau-Nippissing Road. It represents a typical home built by the first settlers.

jubilee edition of 1950, which the company owned. It proved to be the clincher. Contained in the special edition was a column written by a Mrs. Margaret Mitchell. In it, she quoted from an *Arrow* article written back on Friday, January 1, 1885, that described three hotels being in business that year. D.F. Burk, H.W. Trimmer and the Cataract House. "Robert Thompson had a livery stable on Ontario Street, close to the hotel."[1]

That hotel next to which Thompson had his business, was none other than H.W. Trimmer's. The mystery had been solved! Trimmer's Hotel occupied the site of the present day Hotel Central and the pine log unearthed by Borgford turned out to be a foundation pier for Thompson's livery stable! Just as the elderly woman had pointed out earlier on in Kirk-White's investigation. Now the guess was that the gin bottle was probably used to carry water to the horses stabled at Thompson's!

As one door is opened, another is closed. There is unfortunately no record of what happened to Trimmer's Hotel. Did it burn? Or was it simply torn down to make room for James Sharpe's fancy Clifton House in 1887? The first mystery may have been solved, but the great pine pier was for some reason, put back into its grave and covered over by new pavement, As for the infamous green gin bottle? Well, it mysteriously disappeared without a trace.[2]

12 | Angus Kennedy 'Long Live He'

The winter of 1879 was particularly harsh and even rail travel was hampered as locomotives were unable to plow through the huge snowdrifts. To the settlers, it seemed as if the snow was never going to stop falling. However, against all odds of success, leaving his wife and family behind, Angus Kennedy Sr. joined the migration north in the dead of winter. He made the decision to take the couple's eldest son John with him as the purpose of the trip was to stake the family's claim on lots 11 and 12 in Armour Township. The Kennedy land claim lay north of Frank Burk's new settlement and, to get there, the men travelled on foot from Gravenhurst, arriving at their destination on January 1, 1879. In the meanwhile back home in Emily, a community near Peterborough, Angus' wife, Isabelle (Haggart) Kennedy, was busy making preparations to move the rest of the family north. As it turned out, Isabelle and the children had to take the train from nearby Bethany (Durham County) to Gravenhurst, a rail journey that would take a whole two days. She was determined to join her husband in the north as soon as possible, but because of unforeseen delays, by the time the family headed out, it was already the middle of March. Mrs. Kennedy, accompanied by her sons Angus Jr., 20, William Bain 'Bill', 14, and daughters Annie and Jennie, made the last leg of the journey from Gravenhurst by horse drawn sleigh. From the information available, it remains unclear as to the exact ages of Isabelle's daughters at this time, but it is presumed that they were fairly young.[1] It was to take the family an entire week to travel from Gravenhurst to Burk's Falls. Once there, they were greeted by four feet of snow on the ground—a less than welcoming reception![2]

When the Kennedys arrived in the district, the community of Burk's Falls was nothing more than a grouping of shanties which could be counted on the fingers of one hand. The surrounding countryside had an equal number of settlers. But as it so happened there was not one single merchant among them. In order to obtain necessary supplies, the Kennedys, like most area settlers, were forced to take bimonthly trips to the closest general store located in Katrine. Since the last whistle stop was Gravenhurst, some 60 miles away, it was only on a rare occasion that a settler would take on the task of travelling south, and when they did, that purchase had to be extra special.[3]

The Kennedy's first home was no cabin in the woods but a fine two story, hewn log house. With the sons all taking on steady paying jobs with local lumber companies, Angus Sr. and Isabelle were able to purchase six head of cattle and a team of horses in a relatively short time.

Their closest neighbours, John Cowie and his family, and the Brimacombe brothers, John Henry, William Metherell, Samuel and Albert, lived on adjoining lots. Both the Cowies and Brimacombes hailed from the town of St. Mary's in south-western Ontario. Arriving in 1877 ahead of Cowie, the Brimacombes, being the neighbourly type that they were, built the Cowie's log house for them. John Henry and Albert settled in the 'Old Berriedale' area which, in the early days, was nothing more than a general boundary area between Strong and Armour townships, near what was referred to locally as 'the hill.' Eventually a

Social functions played an important part in the lives of early residents of Almaguin. Pictured here is a community gathering in Burk's Falls. The date of the photograph is unknown, but judging by the style of clothing worn by the residents, the picture was most likely taken before WWI.

community took root here and acquired the name of Berriedale.[4] (Unfortunately for modern-day researchers, the early settlers took the origins of the name to the grave with them.) While the other brothers decided to spread out a bit into nearby Strong Township, it was William who decided to send for their mother and father, John and Jane Brimacombe and sister Ellen Jane. By the close of 1881, they had all settled in with him.[5]

As more pioneers moved into the area, settlements began to fan out in a northerly direction. Those settling in Stirling Falls kept their ties with nearby Berriedale. One of the first to stake a claim here was John Milne, a free grant settler who eventually gained title to his 100 aces on October 5, 1882. Milne arrived in the area in September of 1877, leaving his home in the village of Ethel, located in south-western Ontario's Huron County near Brussels. Accompanied by his uncle Will, he boarded one of the regular steamers heading north from Gravenhurst to Rosseau and from there took the stagecoach to Magnetawan. At this point, nephew and uncle had no other option but to walk the remaining way through the woods in a north-east direction to Stirling Falls. To keep them moving in the right direction, the men relied on the sound of the rushing water which could be heard from a great distance away.

Some time later John Milne's wife Eliza and the rest of the family, joined them. Unfortunately for Eliza, like Isabelle Kennedy she too had to endure the ravages of the winter weather conditions of 1879. Once in Gravenhurst, it apparently took both of J.T. Haroir's sleighs to accommodate Eliza Milne's possessions and move her family up to their homestead in Stirling Falls.[6]

Taking full advantage of the new opportunities, John Milne set up his own lumber and shingle mill. A short time later, more of the Milne clan arrived. In 1881 Jim and Ellen Milne settled in and built the community's first grist mill. However, when the railway finally pushed north from Gravenhurst and bypassed Stirling Falls, most of the Milnes pulled up stakes and moved out. Jim sold his grist mill to John Blain and relocated to the northern settlement of Powassan while John Milne went south to Huntsville. By 1892, the enterprising firm of John Milne & Son Huntsville Planing Mills turned out large quantities of doors, frames, sash, mouldings, dressed lumber and interior finish of all shapes and sizes. Milne's operation also handled small household items such as broom handles and chair stock.[7]

With business being so brisk, Milne immediately decided to enlarge the planing mill and promptly installed a new engine and boiler. According to the advertisements of the time, summer residents wanting building materials for cottage construction, could pick up whatever they needed at a moment's notice at Milne's Planing Mills. And then, almost as quickly as John Milne had established his flourishing business, it was all over. A fire in 1893 completely destroyed the plant and once again Milne was forced to uproot his family. This time he headed south of the border to Cleveland, Tennessee. It was here that he established another successful business, a chair factory. So successful was the new enterprise that, as the couple grew homesick, there was enough money for John and Eliza to return to the Burk's Falls area in some comfort. Milne's sons took over the Tennessee factory and continued the operation.[8]

Despite the incredible hardships, these early settlers were an unbelievably resilient lot and most lived to an old age. The sons and daughters of Angus Kennedy Sr. were among those blessed with this longevity. Angus Jr. died at the age of 96 on January 12, 1956 at his home in Burk's Falls. Throughout his long life he enjoyed reading the *Toronto Globe*, beginning at the time when it was printed as a weekly in the 1800s.[9] His brother Bill who died in 1950 at the Burk's Falls Red Cross Hospital at the age of 85, like the rest of the men in the family, had been lumberman all his life.[10] Although Bill was the youngest of the Kennedy children, the family farm was passed down to him when he decided to get married at a fairly early age. Marrying Jean Cowie of nearby Stirling Falls, the couple had two children, Archie and Ina, but unfortunately, their daughter died in infancy. There is no record of what actually became of Jean, but we are told that in 1903, Bill got married again, this time to Jean Bolton. She died unexpectedly in 1921, leaving him with a stepdaughter, Verena.[11]

Throughout his lifetime, Bill only lived about a dozen years at the family farm in Berriedale, but during that time the farmhouse became the centre of community life, doubling at times as a hall for church suppers and prayer meetings, as well as the occasional party. With only fifteen to twenty family farms spread over a vast area, even the simplest get-togethers took on a certain importance. It was a full, satisfying life for the area's young. 'Sugaring off' sprees, Halloween raids and other excuses for fun and excitement were common events.[12]

Telephones didn't exist, but the news travelled exceptionally well, usually by word of mouth. It didn't take very long to round up the young folk for square dances, lasting 'til the first light of day. Although the area produced plenty of fiddlers up at 'Old Berriedale,' Ab Brimacombe was generally the first to 'tune up a reel.' Despite the hard work, life had many good moments in those early days, with community picnics being the highlight of the summer. A dancing platform would be set up, and ball games and horse-racing were viewed as the most important events at these gatherings. The Berriedale boys seldom took a back seat to anyone when it came to shenanigans at these affairs. But the Kennedy boys, it has been said, did their share.

Even in later life, after Angus Kennedy Jr. gave up the rigors of being a river driver in 1893 and moved to Burk's Falls, the Kennedy legend followed him. A.R. Fawcett, editor of the *Burk's Falls Arrow* and booster of the town, once burst out into poetry in his own newspaper after Angus Kennedy, by now a Fire Chief, brought glory to the community. Fawcett had purchased the *Arrow* from F.W. (or R.W.) Sieveright back in 1905, after leaving his post at the weekly newspaper, *Leader and Recorder*, which served Toronto Junction.[13] Along with his fire brigade, Kennedy took top honours at the 1913 competition staged in Orillia for area fire fighters. This outstanding achievement brought the winning banner and $100 back to Burk's Falls that year, on July 31.

> 'Now let us sing "Long Live the King"
> And Angus Kennedy, long live he,
> And when our chief next goes abroad,
> May I be there to see.'

Sadly, the only landmarks of the old Kennedy homestead in 'Old Berriedale' are a few lilac bushes, both white and mauve, with nothing to be seen of the farmhouse and barn now long gone. A view so different from the earlier days when the rafters of both often rang with the music of fiddlers, young happy voices and the rhythm of dancing feet.[14]

Someone had fond memories of the Berriedale area and penned the following poem. Regrettably neither the author nor the date of publication are known.[15]

OLD BERRIEDALE

> "Friend Issac Wilson I've just seen
>   your poem on Berriedale,
> Which brings to memory many
>   scenes upon life's backward trail!
> The many hills and lakes, and streams
>   the deer and hunters bound
> But best of all the friends we loved
>   in dear old Parry Sound.
>
> The raisings and the logging bees we
>   used to have, you know
> When we at night were fain to tip,
>   the "light fantastic toe."
> But rheumatic has struck our joints,
>   our day for that is o'ver
> And now a set of "beardless sprigs"
>   will no doubt hold the floor.
>
> While we in words with wisdom fraught
>   will talk of other days,
> When with a pack upon our back
>   we'd follow up the blaze,
> Or fell the spruce and lofty pine, or
>   birch and maple trees.
> And, Oh! the wonders we performed
>   us prime old used-to-bees.
>
> Will Kennedy, and how is he; the
>   Angs ' Booth Black and Read?
> And Jack, the old time lumberman,
>   is he alive or dead?
> And have Milnes all pulled out, and
>   gone—well let me see
> To Halifax, or New Orleans? oh
>   yes, to Tennessee.

And Smith is he still on the trail; with
  long though silent stride
To nip the unsuspecting buck and
  tan his precious hide;
Elizah must be getting on? I'm sure
  his locks are gray,
But then, you know the saying
  "Each dog must have his day."

The Lambs, and William Brimacombe
  and Ab., who pied the bow?
And Jack? Whose home was near
  the Dale—but Sam has gone you
  know,
Upon the hill at Berriedale, "God's
  acre" holds you know
Some of the dearest friends we knew,
  in days of long ago.

Auld Ang. and Laughlin Kennedy,
  and Cowies three or four—
Have joined the great majority upon
  the other shore,
And others, but the heart grows sad,
  their memory brings us pain,
Yet still we hope beyond the veil to
  meet them all again.

And soon my friend the time may
  come when we must heed the call,
Not even Gotch could wrestle Death
  Time "plays the deuce" with all
But we will keep our spirits green
  'till every dog is hung,
And may we never 'ere forget the
  days when we were young."[16]

13 | An Ill Wind

"In A High Windstorm—Flames Rushed Over Main Street of Town" ran a special dispatch to the *Globe*.[1] These headlines were how the rest of the province would hear about the devastating fire in Burk's Falls in the summer of 1908. It not only razed the business section of the little village, but sent $150,000 in real estate up in smoke. The insurance, totalling $70,000, was not enough even to cover the replacement value of the buildings, let alone the contents. Since many merchants of the time lived in quarters above their businesses, their losses were to be two-fold.

It was not the first time 'The Fates' had been tempted. Just three years previously, at the first light of dawn on a stark and frigid February day, another fire had threatened to destroy the thriving community. Both fires originated at the Knight Bros. Co. Sash and Door Factory located on the south banks of the Magnetawan River. In 1905 factory officials claimed that the fire had started somewhere between the kiln and the engine room. The source of the next fire, the one that made headline news around the province, was in the drying kiln itself.[2]

On June 20 1908, while the fire brigade was making rapid progress in dealing with the blaze at the factory itself, an ominous northwest wind went unnoticed. Eye witnesses stated that the wind was very strong that afternoon, but not considered anything out of the ordinary. For this reason apparently no one fighting the factory fire paid much attention to it. Before anyone realized what was happening, that unnoticed wind had whipped flames from the factory to the main street. Those flames swept rapidly along Ontario Street, consuming everything in its path, despite the valiant efforts of the community.

An emergency dispatch was sent to Huntsville and immediately a special train was sent northwards carrying that town's fire brigade and equipment. The additional support did much to hamper the spread of the conflagration and by 9 o'clock at night, the fire was just about extinguished. However, by this time, over thirty businesses and residences had been reduced to nothing more than a smoking rubble. Even the telegraph wires leading into town had been burnt out.[3]

One of the eye witnesses to the terrible fire was Charlie Pettitt of the nearby community of Chetwynd. While only 19 years of age at the time, he never forgot the devastation caused by the blaze. It had become a routine for him to walk the twelve miles west to Burk's Falls on a daily basis, including on that day in June. In later years, he would often pause and reflect on that afternoon. "Everything in Burk's Falls was levelled except for the drug store and Fowler's Store. Everyone said the fire began from the factory. It probably wouldn't have been so bad if there hadn't been a wind. It was so windy that day, it started the whole works going."[4]

Just five years previous, Angus Kennedy and James Wilson had gone into partnership with the purchase of Ike Wilson's livery barn. Combining it with the Burk's Falls Transfer Station, it was to turn into a profitable venture for the partners. Two of their biggest clients were the Knight Bros. Co. Sash and Door Factory and the Tannery, managed by R. J. Watson. Kennedy eventually decided to buy the impressive home of Ike Watson on Copeland Street, right behind the livery barn. Ike Watson was one of many important businessmen in the community at the time. The fire of 1908 that had set the town ablaze, reducing the majority of frame and wooden buildings to ashes, included the livery barn and Kennedy's residence as well. After the fire, a large brick livery and feed barn was constructed on the site and the partners continued on with the business until 1913. The brick livery exists today and is now occupied by Thompson's Machine Shop.[5]

Another important business destroyed in that fire, was that of J. N. Dodd, the village's harness maker. In 1881, while running a profitable business in Katrine, he was appointed treasurer for Armour Township. Relocating to Burk's Falls in 1886, he was able to supplement his harness making by stocking a large selection of boots and shoes. By this time, he was also a recognized dealer in wool and an agent for the Bracebridge Woollen Mills. His business, up to the time of the fire, extended for a radius of more than 50 miles around Burk's Falls.[6]

Businesses burned out in June, 1908:
    Knight Bros. lime kiln
    Burk House
    Clifton House
    R.A. & J. Lamb and
        Smith Butchers and Grocers
    Stables behind butcher shop
    Geo Gilbert Shoe Store
    P.W. Clark Hardware
    A. Culberts & Bligh (Blyth)
        Butchers
    George Culbert Boots and Shoes
    C.W. Coulter General Store
    Kirk & R.J. McDougall, Barbers,
        Poolroom, residence
    S.T. Vanstone Jewellers
    F. Revalin (Reavellin)
        Restaurant
    J.J. Mitchell Candy Store
    H. Rutter Boarding House

    S. (J) Davidovitch General Store
    J.W. Harris, Barber and Tailor
    H. A. Sidier, 'Sydies' (Sydia) General Store
    E.E. Seibers (Lebers) Photography Gallery
    Bennett Bakery
    Stewart's Livery
    Robert Moir's Stables
    Alex Campbell Blacksmith Shop
    Burk's Falls Transfer Company's Livery
    J.N. Dodd, Harness Maker

Homes destroyed:
    Angus Kennedy
    William Lehman
    Thomas Brown
    Ben McClelland
    William Schroeder

Buildings suffering damage:
    W. Sharpe Co. General Store
    Dr. A.W. Partridge (office)
    Arrow Printing Office
    J.P. Fowler General Merchant
    Post Office and CPR ticket office[7]

Back in February of 1905, the time of the first big fire, weather conditions again had played a big role in the outcome. Because of the cold temperatures, the closest fire hydrant to the Knight Bros. Co. Sash and Door Factory was frozen solid. Within twenty minutes of the factory whistle and fire bell sounding the alarm, hundreds of alarmed residents had rushed to the scene. The fire brigade arrived almost as quickly, armed with reels and hoses, but the men were helpless as no water, not even a trickle, would come out of the hydrant. With the factory filled to overflowing with spring shipments of flooring and building materials, all very flammable, little could be saved. To make matters worse, eight carloads of flooring ready to be shipped were burned on the spot. With not a railcar in sight to transport the material to a safe distance, the factory and con-

The Burk's Falls fire of June 20, 1908 wiped out the main business section of town. By 9 o'clock that night, over 30 buildings containing homes and stores had been reduced to rubble. The view seen here is the south-east side of the main street. Even the telegraph wires had been burnt out.

After the great fire of 1908 which razed most of the business section of Burk's Falls, one of the few buildings to survive was the hardware and barber shop, third building from the right. In rebuilding the businesses on the main street, many were fireproofed with the use of brick. Unfortunately, the main street as it is pictured here, no longer exists as several of the buildings had 'mock' fronts added, or were replaced.

tents were in ashes within two hours, all because of a frozen fire hydrant.[8] Total estimate of damage came to $25,000. The villagers took comfort in the fact that, thankfully, only one business had been destroyed and that the community itself had been spared. Everything returned to normal remarkably quickly.

By 1908 daily life in this spirited community had become so routine, that even rowdyism became, once again, a daily occurrence. At the beginning of April, a local resident by the name of John Mckinnon was fined $5.25 for using profane language in the dining room of the famous Clifton House. The arrest was to make headlines. "Authorities were determined to put a stop to swearing and rowdyism and there were thoughts of Parry Sound constables taking some of the altogether too frequent swearers into custody and have the Police Magistrate teaching them manners."[9]

Then on Saturday June 20, 1908, things fell apart all over again. The Clifton House where Mckinnon had been arrested, the Burk House, as well as scores of other businesses, became no more. Ironically, this time around the newly rebuilt Knight Bros Co. Sash and Door Factory was saved from fire by the valiant efforts of the fire brigade and employees, who believed they had learned a valuable lesson from three years previous...or so everyone thought.

14 | Dick the Bummer

By the mid 1860s, the Rosseau-Nipissing Colonization Road had become the first real access into the newly opened District of Parry Sound. Since paying jobs were scarce during this time, economics played a key role for pushing further into the wilderness where it was cheaper to live. More than one settler found the courage to venture on, even after they reached Magnetawan.

For trapper, Richard Mannering, his trek along the colonization road was to make history. After convincing his friend, an Englishman named Alfred Russell, to join him one particular winter for trapping in the wilds, the pair set off from Magnetawan stopping fifteen miles up the road at a campsite set up by teamsters. They discovered the spot to be a regular stopover for men on their way to Nipissing, as it was the half-way point between Magnetawan and Commanda. There were no buildings marking the spot, simply a clearing on the side of the road. It was here that teamsters would tether the oxen and horses to the trees and sleep under their wagons.

As it was to turn out, Richard was not much of a hustler, spending much of his time loafing around when not setting up trap lines. Nicknamed 'Dick the Bummer' by those who got to know this side of him, Richard immediately took a liking to his new name. Before the cold set in, Richard and Alfred built a log cabin in the clearing that was to be in constant use by the pair when not trapping and hunting. As a final touch, Richard proudly hung a shingle upon a nearby tree that had the words 'The Bummer's Roost' emblazoned on it. Dick's' sign, as fate would have it, was to turn

the place into a landmark. In the spring of 1865, a newspaper reporter from Toronto, up in the area to do a story on the colonization road for his publication, came across the signage. Intrigued by his discovery, he filed a write-up on the place, giving it official status.[1] That sign may be long gone, but the location itself continues to be known to this day as Bummer's Roost, thanks to that reporter.

After the newspaperman had left, it dawned on Alfred Russell that this campsite had great potential as a travellers' rest. That summer he began constructing a log boarding house and log stables alongside the cabin the pair had built the year before. After operating successfully as a licensed hotel for the next nine years, its future as a stopping place for settlers heading up the colonization road would continue long afterwards. Eventually Alfred sent for his wife, Maria Henley, and their family grew to include three sons, Edmund, William and Tom.[2] When the Grand Trunk Railway was being surveyed through South River, the surveyors' supplies and equipment were hauled by teams and sleighs from Rosseau along the colonization road to 'Bummer's Roost.' From there to South River they proceeded by dog teams and toboggans over the low-lying lands, crossing Detta and Eagle lakes.

Russell also took charge of the men who were to cut a secondary colonization road westward from 'Bummer's Roost,' to the Great North Road south of Pickerel River. Construction of this road, also known as the North Road or Northern Road, began in 1867 with the intentions of it being used as a link up for wagon trains intent on going from

Parry Sound to Commanda via the Rosseau-Nipissing Colonization Road. Its main purpose was to draw settlers away from established communities, deeper into the new territory. There always has been the belief that the provincial land surveyor at the time, J.W. Fitzgerald, chose the route for the Great North Road by simply appropriating an Indian trail for the purpose. The road itself was to be 14 feet wide and, in hilly sections, a couple of feet wider at 40 rod intervals, (in excess of 80 feet) to admit the passage of teams. Today there are still some traces of the original road in spots where it is not buried under the paved traffic artery. The road ultimately became Highway 124.[3]

This secondary colonization road built under Russell's direction, was to become known as the 'Poor Man's Road', because of the hard work required and the method in which the men were paid. With not even one cross-cut saw among them, the men felled the trees with axes and cut them into the required short lengths. To roll the logs off the roadway, homemade handspikes were used. For long hours of hard labour, the men received in the way of a monthly payment, a $10 voucher for goods at the general store in Magnetawan.

As for Richard Mannering, he seems to have disappeared into the annals of time. One can only presume he continued on as a trapper—'bumming' around in his spare time.

15 | **Dark Doings at Dufferin**

Strategically located in the middle of the thirty-four mile stretch between Rosseau and Magnetawan sat the bustling community of Dufferin Bridge, the first settlement north of Sequin Falls that travellers would encounter as they made their way up the Rosseau-Nipissing Road. A building boom started in the spring of 1879 when the founder of the community, John Clarke, threw open the doors of his newly constructed Dufferin House. Clark was determined to make it a first class hotel and hoped that by going into partnership with his friend Joseph Irwin, it would be supported by the local residents. And why shouldn't it? After all, Irwin had hotel experience at Parry Harbour's Thomson House—and Clark needed that expertise order to make his business venture a success.[1]

However, the Dufferin House soon was to have unexpected competition, coming from no less than a family member of Clark's partner! In less than two months after the official opening of Dufferin House, Richard Irwin's hotel was in operation, just in time for the Orange Day parade on July 12. With the stores in Dufferin Bridge closed for the day while the hotels were open, just about everyone in the settlement had a chance to participate in the festivities. Able to provide all the delicacies and beverages of the season, Richard Irwin's clever manoeuvring of his grand opening turned out to be a smashing success. A dancing platform was erected outside the Irwin Hotel and a German band hired to provide the music. Band members had to travel all the way up from Ten Mile Lake, a considerable distance away, just for the occasion! Guests who grew tired from all the dancing had the option of resting on any one of a number of swings set up around Irwin's hotel. The celebrations of 'The Glorious Twelfth' were to last until almost midnight, when the weary finally packed up their dancing shoes and headed home.[2]

The opening of these two new hotels in Dufferin Bridge that year, added significantly to the number of roadside inns which had popped up along the colonization roads between Bracebridge and Nipissing. According to one newspaper report, "...there was now a beer agent to every three miles—to say nothing of Huntsville and other localities. Must be the unusually dry weather."[3]

Buoyed by such success with two hotels, by August the residents were looking at ways to connect their community with other settlements. Since the Orange Hall located just north of Dufferin Bridge was used by many of the area's settlers, construction was begun on a road network going west towards Parry Sound. Joseph Hall was the one given the go ahead, to oversee the work on the first section, which was named, appropriately enough, the Orange Valley Road. The Orange Hall itself was to sit at the cross-roads![4]

In the meantime, the enterprising Richard Irwin, not content with being just a hotel owner, by late summer had opened up a sawmill. As luck would have it, its opening coincided with the postmaster's plans for a new post office to be designed in the grand Muskoka Gothic style. Once the sawmill was able to provide seemingly unlimited quantities of lumber, a magnificent building was erected according to the postmaster's specifications. So impressed by their new post office were the

Settlers in Almaguin were ill equipped to fight off epidemics. Doctors were few and far between and medicine was primitive at best. One of the most famous tombstones on the Rosseau-Nipissing Colonization Road sits in the Dufferin Bridge Methodist Cemetery. Victims of influenza, six of the seven Morden children died within days of each other, in January of 1902.

villagers, that they were convinced that Dufferin Bridge would soon reach city-status.[5] However, the tranquil days of summer and grand thoughts of a city on the Rosseau-Nipissing Road were to be overshadowed by two startling events—a daring case of attempted highway robbery followed on the heels by a scandal of epic proportions.[6]

Whether the two Frenchmen were actual highwaymen, no one knew for sure as their identity was never revealed. What was for certain was that the victim, a new settler travelling on foot through the area, was to receive a greeting he'd soon not forget! And it was to happen right on the outskirts of Dufferin Bridge. Carelessly flashing his money about while stopping at the numerous roadside inns, the settler became an easy mark once spotted by the two Frenchmen. The duo, watching the man's activities closely, followed him from a safe distance all the way up to Dufferin Bridge. Imbibing in 'blue ruin' along the way didn't help the situation and, by the time the

settler arrived at the community on that fateful day during the first week of August, he was dead drunk.

The stranger's stay in Dufferin Bridge was short and by nightfall the next day, he was back on the road headed north. The Frenchmen tracked the settler to a secluded section of the roadway and confronted him. An attempt by one of the highwaymen to knock the man out may have succeeded if his companion suddenly had not wanted out of the deal. The settler's screams for help after the one robber grabbed his cash quickly brought three local men to the scene, taking the thieves by surprise. Unable to make a quick getaway, the plunderers attempted to hide the loot, but their efforts were thwarted by the rescuers. The struggle that followed sent money scattering all over the road. Lanterns were brought to the scene, the money recovered and returned to the settler.

Ironically, the two Frenchman were allowed to leave Dufferin Bridge in the morning on the promise that they would never return. The general concensus of residents was that since the money had been recovered and no serious injury was sustained by the victim, there was no need to pursue the matter any further.

The second incident followed closely on the footsteps of the attempted highway robbery. It was a tragic affair fueled by local gossip. And at the end of the whole ordeal, unanimous opinion once again won out. "If it gave residents of the community something to talk about, 'Why, whar's the Dufferins?'"[7]

It truly was a nasty bit of business, involving a young woman of questionable morals. Whispers floated through the air every time she walked down the street, but her name was never uttered. And when she suddenly left one day, the more virtuous minded women of the community began to speculate that her vulgar, promiscuous ways had finally caught up with her. There had been rumours of the woman being 'in a family way,' and that's why she had to leave. Such talk certainly made her return to Dufferin Bridge a few months later without a child, all the more shocking. Days after she arrived home, a farewell party hosted by a Mr. R. Gainsford took place at Richard Irwin's hotel. Acting as if nothing had ever happened, the young woman made her grand entrance at the ball.[8] The party was for Edward Wood, a respected local farmer who had made plans to go to Ottawa after selling his homestead to a Mr. Edwards of Ballenthraw, Ireland. Over sixty of his friends and acquaintances, including the young woman, attended the festivities on August 12. The party lasted well into the night, right up until 6 o'clock the next morning. Predictably, the young woman's brazen conduct proved irresistible to the gentlemen in attendance. Infuriated by the situation and left sitting with unfilled dance cards, the other ladies were determined to set things right. With nothing else to do but watch, a scheme was hatched that same night, designed to humiliate the shameless young hussy.

A charge of "concealment of birth" was laid before a Justice of the Peace the next day and a warrant sworn out for the woman. It had been discovered, through discreet inquiries at the ball, that the reason no one had seen her with the baby was because it was dead. A coroner's jury was summoned to enquire into the reasons for the death. Dark hints of murder were ruled as gossip and immediately thrown out at the inquiry. However, after much fuss and examination and after a number of witnesses, including the ladies from Gainsford's party, had been sworn in and had testified on matters they knew absolutely nothing about, the inquiry was adjourned. It was decided a proper medical man was needed to sort out the truth. Dr. Mackenzie, who had volunteered as coroner

in the case, eventually threw his hands up in despair and declared he could not shed any light on the situation either! The baby had been found buried, wrapped up in an old apron and a piece of newspaper, and quite possibly may have died, according to the doctor, from natural causes. The young woman's mother, testified that the baby had indeed been born alive, but died a short while after birth. Utimately, the jury returned a verdict of "found dead, but from causes which there was no evidence to show."[9]

Life eventually returned to normal. John Clark, deciding to leave the hotel business in Dufferin Bridge, moved seventeen miles north to Magnetawan with the prospects of starting over again. By the middle of October, Clark still with his partner Joseph Irwin, had taken over a hotel run by Donald Ross, an easy acquisition since Ross was returning to his farm in Christie Township.[10] While Clark was busy settling into the new business, his daughter Mary was busy with wedding plans. She had accepted a proposal from the new proprietor of the Dufferin House, James Perkin. Their wedding, held at her father's former hotel, turned into a grand ball. With guests expected to arrive at a steady pace all day long, from Rosseau and points beyond, a fatted calf was killed and served at the wedding supper.[11]

The good life in Dufferin Bridge for Mary and James Perkin and the others, was to be only temporary. One of five communities between Rosseau and Magnetawan which prospered as the stream of settlers continued, Dufferin Bridge slowly lost its reason for being once the railways moved in and the road traffic dried up.[12] Desperation set in as townsfolk left one by one. By the turn of the century, the population of Dufferin Bridge had dwindled to just 65. Out of the remaining businesses that had blossomed over the previous twenty years previous, only a few remained. The community barely managed to hang on to its post office, run by Martha Beckett Vigrass, the widow of James Vigrass. Of the hotels, Irwin's Hotel remained, now operated by Thomas Scott. The last general store left in Dufferin Bridge was operated by S. Plumtree while Thomas Vickers owned the only remaining grocery store.[13]

Time had not been good to the community that once had aspired city status. The remaining residents, battered by the harsh climate and poor soil, had no strength left to withstand the onslaught of sweeping epidemics at the turn of the century. Cemetery populations soon outgrew that of the community.

Hardest hit by the Influenza epidemic of 1902 was the Morden family. Shortly after the New Year and within a span of one week, James Morden and his wife, Janey, buried six of their seven young children in the community's Methodist Cemetery. The Morden homestead may have been just one mile away from Dufferin Bridge, but there was no doctor in town and no medicine, leaving only two parents dealing with their grief in isolation. By January 14, their son Charles, age four years, nine months, was dead. Within the next six days the children died one by one. On January 15, Earle, who was almost three, passed away, followed by his brother Albert, age six

years, four months. Ellamanda, age seven, died on January 18, followed by her sister Minnie, age ten and a half. When Janey's baby, one and a half year old Dorcas, died in her arms, it was finally all over.

Devastated, James packed up his wife and remaining child, Lucinda, 12, and left Dufferin Bridge as soon as weather permitted. Their destination was Detroit. Although Janey was to have one more daughter in 1905, she never recovered from the tragic loss of her other children. Her doctor's prescription of Laudanum, widely used as a nerve remedy at the time, was concocted of tincture of opium steeped in wine spirits. Janey eventually became addicted and died ten years later of a drug overdose.

As for the Morden's oldest daughter, Lucinda, records show that she married and apparently returned to Ontario to settle with her husband in Uxbridge. She died in 1992 at the age of 102.[14] Little is known of what happened to the Morden baby born in 1905, or for that matter, James Morden after the death of his wife.

Dufferin Bridge continued to wither until it was reclaimed by the land itself and today, all that remains of this once prosperous community, are two cemeteries, one with the large tombstone that marked the tragic passing of the Morden children.

16 | The Twelfth of July

Before the turn of the century, the Twelfth of July was 'The Big Day' of summer for most in the province, including residents of Almaguin. It was not an official holiday, but when all the Orangemen took time off for their annual celebration, not enough workers were left to run the mills and businesses. So a holiday it became! The fraternity began as a secret society instituted in Ireland in 1795, to uphold Protestant control of government and oppose the Catholic religion and influence. Its membership was to reach far into the new world and well into the 19th century. Almost every town and hamlet boasted an Orange Hall in those days, a building which served as the focal point of the community. Council meetings were held in the Orange Hall, as well as concerts and dances and box socials.

The following are just a few examples of how this important event was marked by residents of Almaguin. From Huntsville to North Bay, the Twelfth of July was celebrated on a rotation system which meant gathering in a different town each year. On the special day, thousands flocked to the lucky site from near and far. To transport so many faithful, railway officials made certain that special trains were running. Sometimes up to twelve coaches were needed to accommodate all the people. As each community had its own fife and drum band, throughout the day, the air would be vibrant with the boom of the big drums and the shrill squeal of the fifes.[1]

Besides the bands, sports were also a big part of the Twelfth. As an example, in 1885 the celebrations were held in Dunchurch. Shooting, racing, jumping, rowing, paddling and saw log riding kept the attention of the people until well into the early morning hours. Some of the more prominent winners were G. Kelley, P. Andrews, J. North, H. Calvert, and J. Millen. On this particular Twelfth of July, three things were proven to the satisfaction of the residents of Dunchurch. According to the report in the *Parry Sound North Star*, those three things were; first, that grey horses can indeed swim, second, that brothers cling together in a saw log race, and third, that a robin will sometimes take to the water like a duck![2]

In another example, four years later in 1899, soccer had taken over as the predominant sport on the Glorious Twelfth. Teams from Huntsville to North Bay would take part in the competitions, but they were no match for the Trout Creek entry which generally won the championship. The team included three members of the well known Trussler family—brothers Gilbert, Albert and James.[3]

Such celebrations would continue into the twentieth century and gradually become less of a focal point in community life as other purposes evolved.

All of these towns took great pride in their communities. The picturesque community of Dunchurch, located on Highway 124 west of Magnetawan, continues to be one of the prettiest little hamlets on the western boundaries of the Almaguin Highlands. Like many of the villages, the past held great promise for the community as the population continued to grow under government incentives. The following poem clearly illustrates the strong convictions of its citizens at the time.[4]

DUNCHURCH

"Dunchurch, our fair little town, is pretty
   hard to beat,
      We have three good general merchants
      who neither lie nor cheat,
Of course they are well instructed and they
      can't go far astray,
      While they've three good faithful parsons
      to help them on their way.

Our town is very healthy, so our doctor gets
      no show,
      If it were not for some accidents, our
      M.D. would have to go;
That is why our undertaker must two busi-
      nesses combine,
      And he makes most all his money along
      the other line.

Our merchant men are hustlers and do busi-
      ness every day,
      It is men like these in any town who will
      make their business pay.
      Of course we have a butcher, for we sure
      ly must have meat,
You will always find when in our town you'll
      get something good to eat.

We have a worthy blacksmith who is a stal-
      wart man and strong,
      And we don't forget our teacher, for he's
      been here so long,
For our scholars are the smartest that you'll
      find anywhere,
      I tell you when they go from home they
      make this old world stare.

We have a shoemaker and a barber, who do
      their work up fine,
      And we don't owe Andrew Carnegie in
      the Public Library line!

For our people are independent, and they have
      got the tin,
      Why we will have to get the Sovereign
      Bank to keep our money in.

The harness man is located near the middle of
      the town,
      And he sells just heaps of harness to the
      people all around.
Our saw mill keeps a humming from daylight
      until dark,
      She keeps all hands a humping to keep
      away the plank.

Did you ever meet our busmen they are men
      of wide renown,
      They keep the smartest turnouts to be
      found in any town.
They make their trips quite regular to Ahmic
      Harbour and the Sound,
      And their horses can't be beaten in the
      country all around.

There are lumbermen and farmers and agents
      here galore,
      And I really do not think it wise to tell you
      any more.
Only if we had a railway this would be a city
      soon,
      For a railway is really all we need to make
      this old town boom.

It is next thing to impossible, in an article
      so small,
      To tell you of the Whitestone stage and the
      boarding houses all,
But of course with all this business it is hard
      to keep in line,
And our teamsters are fairly rushed to death
      hauling goods in all the time."[5]

17 | Cat Famine

In the early days when settlers were few in the district, there came a time of a cat famine. Superstition was set aside completely, for next to his oxen and his wife, the poor settler valued his cat. In fact, if he possessed all three he was considered pretty well to do. The plaintive meow-meow was considered music for the soul for such was a guarantee against finding socks and overalls perforated before morning, the bits gone to furnish bedding for a horde of 'midnight brigands.'[1]

Cats were so essential that the settler had to have one—or move out his dwelling. Beg, borrow, buy, or steal, there were settlers who would "face the penalties of the law by the larceny of a cat."[2]

A routine trip to Magnetawan for groceries, begun on a cold winter's day in the 1870s, was to bring one such early settler the unexpected luck of actually finding a saucy little feline in red. Young Sam McGee of Strong Township was forced to take the long walk through the bush to the general store in Magnetawan, as there were no merchants set up in Sundridge at that time.[3]

It was to take McGee three days to make the round trip journey. When finally he arrived at his destination, McGee spotted a young kitten on the wooden sidewalk on his way to the store. Stooping down to pet it, he noted a red ribbon bow. After going inside and making the necessary purchases, McGee spent a little time warming himself up for the long journey home. The main item he had come for was flour, which he packed for carrying on his shoulders. As for the extra purchase of biscuits and cheese, that was to sustain him on the journey back home.

The kitten had waited, obviously attracted to Sam, and persisted in following him as he started out of town. It certainly looked as if the feline was lost and, McGee, having no time to waste since much of his return trip would be in the cold and the dark, finally thrust the purring little ball of fur deep into the pocket of his long overcoat. Along the way he shared his meager provisions with the passenger and decided that he actually was thankful for the company.

Red Ribbon Kitty was what he called it and, as luck would have it, the kitten happened to be a female. Sam's neighbours, the Cates, had a male cat. When litters of kittens began arriving sometime later, the township pioneers were overjoyed. Their cat famine was over!

However, there was another earlier instance when a settler, driven by the plague of mice, was not so fortunate and who resorted to stealing a cat. That year was 1862 and it was not until twenty-seven years later, that the cat thief confessed his crime to a newspaper reporter with the *Parry Sound North Star*. Known only as N.P. to his readers, his confession ran with the resolve, "If I am tried for the awful crime, I hope my jury will be 17 old settlers who did not own cats."[4]

According to N.P., his actions were governed by extenuating circumstances. In fact, the hundreds of mice running throughout his house totally disrupted the couple's lives. Once his wife had been a patient woman. However, the continual raids on her Sunday garments, which were now being turned to rags, were getting the better of her.

Attempts to borrow a cat proved futile, as

neighbour 'White's' cat was on loan to 'Black' and someone else had the promise of it next. Then one day, N.P.'s luck changed. A distant neighbour residing some ten miles away needed an extra pair of hands. When the settler arrived at the homestead, what did he see but "a beautiful black and yellow cat and a kitten of the same lovely hue playing in front of the house."[5] Visions of his wife's sorrowful eyes as she examined the remains of her best calico gown rose before him, and the settler suddenly discovered the Commandment was broken. He coveted his neighbour's cat!

The first question was how to carry away the plunder. A box was found and hid and the plan hatched to execute the crime the following night. "Cautiously I crept towards the little cot in which my unsuspecting victim lay wrapped in the arms of sleep. I thrust my arm forward. Shades of Lucifer! I though I had fowled on a carding machine, but I hung on and succeeded in bringing out my prize, carried it down and caged it, taking care to put in a piece of bread that I had perloined (sic) from the supper table."[6]

The next day as the settler was getting ready to leave for home, the neighbour's wife whispered something to her husband and they both vanished. Reappearing a half hour later, the wife obviously in distress, informed N.P. that the couple had been planning to give his wife a little kitten as a present. Knowing of the mouse problem in the man's house, the couple had saved the last of the litter for N.P. to take home. But the kitten had mysteriously disappeared!

Guilt ridden but saying nothing, the settler made his good byes and started for home with the kitten safely stowed away. The 'present' was greeted with open arms. Later that evening the only sound that broke the stillness of the night was that made by a young mouse upsetting things as he raced around to keep from being eaten alive. N.P. unable to stand the deception any longer, confessed the whole harrowing tale to his wife the following day. She apparently was barely able able to contain her mirth over her husband's dilemma.

The settler reflected that over the past twenty-seven years at any opportune moment, his wife took the time to remind him of his escapade. For, suffering no more from the plague of mice, the predicament now was a swarm of hungry cats!

18 | The Magnetawan River

A little more than 150 years ago, the area now known as the District of Parry Sound was nothing more than a trackless wilderness. Even surveyors who came to the region in 1870 concluded that although the region consisted of millions of acres of undeveloped land, it was exceptionally heavily timbered. How was anybody going to be convinced to settle in a forest? Luckily for the surveyors, in between the huge tracts of timber there were pockets of arable land that appeared to be suitable for cultivation. And since the government was bent on seeing the new land settled, greater inducements were needed than the free land grants which had been offered since 1853...inducements such as a way to get to the new frontier.[1]

As noted earlier, the first real route to the newly charted territory took the form of a major colonization road begun in 1866 near the Muskoka settlement of Rosseau. It eventually was completed eight years later, carved through 67 miles of virgin forest. The first leg of this road, however, ended at a spot along the South River soon to be settled by incoming pioneers. They adopted the name of the river for their little community. Many other settlements soon cropped up along the new road and the most resilient of the fledgling settlements turned out to be Magnetawan Village, named appropriately enough, for the river on whose banks it stood. Twenty miles upriver another community was created at the falls along the river, by a man named David Francis Burk. Soon, clusters of other smaller hamlets were scattered in between the two, along the banks of the Magnetawan River.[2]

Although Muskoka, by the 1870s had

already been inundated by sportsmen from southern Ontario and the United States who were seeking new challenges, it would not be for another ten years before that interest spilled into Parry Sound. As those numerous settlements began blossoming around Magnetawan Village, it became clear to the government that a lock was required at this point to overcome the rapids. This would, it was reasoned, enable steamers carrying passengers, both sightseers and settlers, as well as freight, to travel the additional ten miles westward to Ahmic Harbour. But before the lock system could be built, the first boat actually to navigate the Magnetawan River for short distances between several communities was the aptly-named *Pioneer*. Built by A.E. Morris of Magnetawan in 1879, surviving records show that the *Pioneer* was a 34 foot long vessel that eventually was joined by a second river steamer. What she looked like is anyone's guess. Some believe that the second ship to run on the river with the *Pioneer* may have been called the *Ada*. However, to this day no one has been able to determine this ship's identity or appearance. All that seems to be known about her is that she was broken up for scrap in 1886. As for the *Pioneer*, she officially disappeared from the record books after 1884.[3]

In September of 1883 the government finally called for tenders for the lock at Magnetawan and, in just three months, the bid of Ottawa contractor, Michael Starrs, was accepted. Ironically, it was because of a timber shortage that the initial work on the lock project faced serious delays. The contract called for the system to be of solid log construction and to occupy no more space than

Everyone loves a summer picnic. The early riverboats on the Magnetawan were used extensively by tourists as well as the local population to get to popular spots along the river between Burk's Falls and Ahmic Harbour. This picture, taken in 1913, is a group of Burk's Falls residents who most likely were on their way to the Midlothian Wharf on the steamer *Wanita*. A young Florence Sharpe stands in the middle, centre row, a young man on her right and on her left, Gladys Cook Dyer, wearing a frilly bonnet.

was necessary to moor boats, scows and timber cribs.[4] It wasn't until the following year that the control dam, an impressive 157 feet in length located at the outlet of Ahmic Lake, was actually completed. However, problems arose once the lower coffer dam was completed and pumps were rigged up to it to drain the basin. They were not strong enough to do the job and new ones had to be substituted.[5] The lock itself, formed of rock-filled timber cribwork, was finished in 1886. It measured 112 feet by 28 feet and provided the exact amount of water over its sills needed to float the large river steamers. In turn, it was flanked by wing-dams of similar construction that were able to raise or lower vessels a distance of approximately ten feet.[6]

With the railway coming through Burk's Falls in 1885, the new transportation service provided a major boost to the steamship business on the Magnetawan. The first recorded ship to pass through the lock was the *Wenonah*, on July 8, 1886. Built the year the lock opened, she was owned and operated by the Muskoka and Nipissing Navigation Company. Not only was she the longest vessel at 94 feet in length, but also the only paddle wheeller vessel ever to run on the river. The longest, yes, but the *Wenonah* did not hold the title of being the largest ship ever to ply the river.

The *Wenonah* had a combination propulsion of paddle wheels and crew, and to manoeuvre this ship down the Magnetawan had to be a masterpiece of piloting. Even today, anyone who has boated along that crooked trail from Burk's Falls to Lake Cecebe, must sit back and admire the men who were able to navigate a 94 foot long vessel down the coiling river bed without running aground. Eventually, in 1906, her paddles were removed while the ship was being refurbished and later the *Wenonah* was navigated solely by crew until 1908 when she mysteriously caught fire on Lake Cecebe and sank.[7] No one ever determined what actually happened, a mystery to this day.

By 1886 another steamer named the *Cecebe*, also owned by the Muskoka Nipissing Navigation Company joined the *Wenonah*. By now the company operated numerous ships on the Muskoka Lakes and was intent on expanding its territory northwards. Only one-third the size of its sister ship, the *Cecebe,* for some unexplained reason, had a short career and ceased running after only four years of service. Again, existing records show that she was doomed for scrap and was broken up around 1896. A third vessel which operated in the system for approximately five years, joined the fleet the same year as the *Cecebe*. It was the little *Lady Katrine* built south of Burk's Falls at the community of Katrine.[8]

The 1890s became the golden years for ship building in Almaguin. In 1890 and in the following year, the *Emulator* and the *Glen Rosa* were built at Magnetawan Village by the Waltons, the most prominent of the steamboat owners operating on the Magnetawan River. However, it appears that both steamers were demolished for scrap by 1908. Another steamship that managed to survive longer than most was the *Cyclone*, built at Ahmic Harbour in 1896. When she was purchased by Albert A. Agar in 1899, she was renamed the *Wanita*. A well known Burk's Falls merchant, Agar was also a prominent local ship owner. While some believe it's unlucky to rename a vessel, it is not known whether it was because of this name change or an accident that caused the former *Cyclone* to burn to the water line while moored at Burk's Falls in December 1911. However, fate was kind to her. She was rebuilt as a tug and continued to operate on the river from 1913 onwards. The *Cyclone* was not the only vessel A.A. Agar was to purchase. He also acquired the *Theresa*, built in 1900 at Rosseau Falls, as well as the *Gravenhurst*, built at her namesake town in 1902. This latest steamer was brought up to the Magnetawan River in 1910.[9]

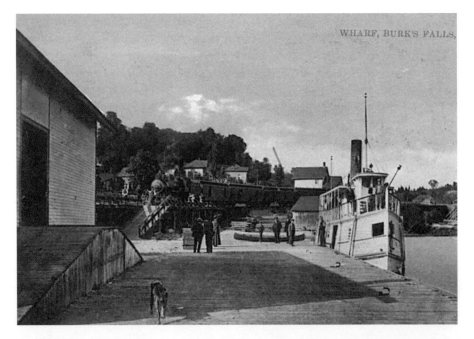

The steamer *Wanita*, pictured here, along with the *Armour*, and the *Gravenhurst*, were operated by the Magnetawan River and Lakes Steamboat Line, eventually owned by A.A. Agar of Burk's Falls. There is no reference to when the *Wanita* was built, but the *Gravenhurst* was built in 1902 and the *Armour* in 1906. The train from Toronto was a common sight in the heyday of riverboats. Most steamers carried both passengers and freight to Magnetawan and Ahmic Harbour.

By far the largest ship of the day was the *Armour*. Grossing 191 tons, she was built at Burk's Falls in 1906. And like so many steamers of her day, the great *Armour* also met a fiery end at Burk's Falls in the early 1930s. However, right to the final days of the local steamship era, the title of longest river steamer on the Magnetawan was retained by the *Wenonah*.[10]

In the twenty-five years between the *Wenonah*'s inaugural voyage down the river and the year 1910, the lock-keeper recorded 17,590 passages of steamers through the system. It worked out to an average of 704 per shipping season. An impressive 511 steamers passed through the locks in 1888 alone. Allan Kennedy was the first lock and bridge keeper to be hired, but unfortunately just eight years later, while on the job, his career was cut short when he fell off the lock. Mortally injured, he was to die from those injuries a short time later. His son Charles assumed his late father's duties and continued in the role of lock and bridge keeper until 1905 when, for unexplained reasons, he resigned.[11] During the Kennedy family's tenure of manning the lock system, the seasonal averages for scows passing through were 181 with 30 cribs of timber.

During the year 1897, extensive repair work was needed and work started on the lock with apparently no interruption to the shipping schedule. According to the existing records, the repairs made included new quoin posts as well as extensive channel clearing. The water course, 100 yards from the boat channel was cleared to a depth of three feet, a width of 28 feet and a length of 198 feet. By the winter of 1910-11, the timber sides of the lock had been completely rebuilt in concrete. Although less picturesque, this replacement structure was thought to require little maintenance, but the engineers were proven wrong. Throughout the long history of the lock system, constant repairs and modifications were made. Masonry dams adjacent to the locks were built in 1923, replacing the wing dams. Then in 1938, the lock gates were replaced only to be replaced again in 1963. Two years later in 1965, more repairs necessitated the lowering of the water level so that the bottom of the lake and the upper part of the lock were exposed. The river bottom revealed a large anchor that was reportedly unearthed by local resident, Joe Bernas. The hull of a large boat, believed to have been once owned by Henderson Troyer, a local Magnetawan butcher, was also spotted at this time.[12]

Thirty years later, in 1995, because of the lock system's deteriorating condition, the provincial government decided to close it down. A decision that would rally a tenacious village reeve and her supporters to challenge the government's decision, making way for the construction of a brand-new lock that was reopened in 1998 to boating traffic.

19 | Era of the River Drives

"After more than half a century, it stands neglected and unoccupied, but just as strong and secure as the day it was built, for the purpose of holding in confinement drunken shantymen, who were plentiful in that era of river drives."[1] So read the *Toronto Globe* report on Magnetawan's one and only public gaol. By the time anyone really took notice of its historical importance, it was already the 1930s and the gaol stored nothing more dangerous in its locked cells than the village's supply of dynamite. Yet when the Ontario government went ahead and built the gaol in 1885, the same year that the Magnetawan River locks were built, it was not because of soaring crime in the area. The construction of the gaol was, in fact, prompted by the community's fear of the shantymen who regularly converged on Magnetawan's two hotels. The 1880s were prosperous times when upwards of 75 to 90 shantymen made fourteen river drives a season, men, who always made it a point to stop in Magnetawan.

The government's contract to build the gaol was awarded to Hugh Miller and Ledge Kennedy who, in turn, hired Francis Stewart for the finishing work inside. Ironically, Stewart, who was township councillor for fifteen years, also got the job as the unpaid gaoler, a position he was to hold for a very long time.[2]

Like many of the communities and waterways in Almaguin, the name Magnetawan was derived from an Indian word. Although over time there has been more than one interpretation of the correct spelling of Magnetawan, there has never been any doubt to its meaning. Magnetawan, as in Magnetawan River, means 'swift flowing water.' In old jour-

nals and survey maps, this vast waterway extending from Algonquin Park to Georgian Bay has been referred to as the 'Maganatawan,' a corruption of the Indian name Mawgawnettewang which means, 'a lost channel,' as well as sometimes being called the Maganettawan, the Magaetawan, the Magenattawan, to say nothing of its present name, Magnetawan. The river was also once referred to as the Neyetawa. According to an unnamed source, Neyetawa was apparently the Indian word for 'swift flowing channel.'[3] As for the present-day spelling of Magnetawan, one can only guess that it evolved over the course of time.

The settlement turned out to be one of those places that seemed to lie dormant for some time before suddenly turning itself into a thriving village. For the incoming pioneer, the only logical choice for a permanent site was where the river narrowed down to a manageable 75 feet. This was to be the only place for miles in either direction, where the river could be bridged or forded.[4] In order to cross the river, the hardy pioneers created a floating log contraption for the first bridge. Of course, it was a bit of a problem whenever a team crossed over since their weight would sink the logs, but once they were on the other side, the bridge would bob back up just as fast as it went down.[5] For William Matthews, one of Magnetawan's earliest pioneers, his timing turned out to be most unfortunate. Arriving on the scene before the floating bridge had been constructed, he had no choice but to force the cattle he had brought with him to swim the river.[6]

By 1870, the surrounding Township of

Chapman had been surveyed for the government by Henry Little, a surveyor who apparently ignored the fact that there had been squatters in the area for quite some time. He also paid little attention to the existing logging camps along the Magnetawan River, those owned by one Samuel Armstrong. These camps as records show, went back as far as 1865 and Armstrong is the one that has been credited with cutting the first winter road from Rosseau to his headquarters on the southern tip of Ahmic Lake.[7] Being able to cadge (carry) in his supplies with horse drawn sleighs, he would distribute them to his various camps by big pointer boats the following summer.

The lumberjacks who worked in Armstrong's camps had to walk in from Rosseau carrying their worldly possessions on their back in 'turkeys' or sacks. Some of the lumberjacks who later settled in the area included: James 'Jim' and Hugh Miller (1885); Hugh Irwin; John and Joe Fluker; Edward Jenkins; Bob Elliott and Sam Best, who later became the crown lands agent at Magnetawan. By 1873, the Dodge Lumber Company was to cut out the Nipissing

Colonization Road from Rosseau to Magnetawan, onward to Lake Nipissing. It was at this point, that Armstrong moved on to the Town of Parry Sound.[8]

Robert Sparks appeared to be the only person to take the squatters into consideration and mapped out Magnetawan with them in mind. The first recorded settler in this area was James Miller, who, as one of Armstrong's lumberjacks, made the trip on foot from Rosseau to Magnetawan in October of 1868.[9] Less than five years later on June 19, 1873, Miller took out a mortgage for $400 with the intention of building a sawmill, yet three years later the village consisted of nothing more than one store and a drafty, roughly built shanty that served to house overnight travellers. By then, Magnetawan did have a crown lands office operated by another former lumberjack, Sam Best, and a permanent shanty owned by Hugh Irwin.

It was not until 1879 however, that the Magnetawan valley experienced its first 'building boom.' That year, two licenced hotels were built, along with a temperance hotel, four general stores, a post office, tin shop and bakery, along with a flour and feed

General stores were the mainstay of early communities, as this one apparently was with its wide array of produce and dry goods. There is still considerable debate over where this store was located—South River or Magnetawan, as well as when it was constructed. Who was the proprietor? If the store was located in South River, then it could have been Boadway's, but no one knows for certain.

store. Even a watchmaker arrived in town. The first sawmill and grist mill had been built in 1878 by John Kennedy and, by the following year, village lots were going for $200 each.[10] The first men to actually open one of the new stores were Bracebridge businessmen, Dill and Shaw. Druggist Donald MacMillan, who came to Magnetawan from Lucknow, Bruce County in 1878, also started keeping a general store. In later years, MacMillan switched to selling drugs and kept a post office on the premises.[11] Magnetawan now also had a school house and three churches on their way to being built or already standing. Records show that construction costs for the Presbyterian Church were $1,500.[12]

In the early 1880s, Kennedy's mill operated as the Purdie Flour Mill, only to burn down just a few years later. Once rebuilt, the mill site changed hands several times that decade. Kennedy sold it to a Mr. McEachern who, in turn, sold it to the Taylor Lumber Co. of Hamilton. The grist mill was then sold separately to John Schade, only to have fire raze it to the ground once more and again it would be reconstructed. Eventually the grist mill was dismantled by Robert and Ernest Daley, to make way for the Daley Electric Plant in 1922.[13] Since the Daleys already had their own grist mill, small sawmill planer and shingle mill nearby, they had no use for this particular mill. Their primary interest was in the water power the site provided.[14] The Daleys, in turn, purchased a 75 kilowatt two-phase, 2,300 volt generator, excitor and switch board which came from High Falls in Powassan. In 1925 they built the cement building which stands to this day.[15] For the next thirty years, hydro-electric power was produced from this location. The former electric plant built on Kennedy's mill site became the local museum in the early 1970s.

Now, back in 1885, despite all of the community's fuss over drunken shantymen, there was reportedly never more than one prisoner in custody at any one time at the gaol, and not one had any kind of 'reputation' to speak of. Nestled in behind the Anglican Church and within a few yards of the main street, the gaol was an impressive building, made of pine logs one foot square, rock bolted and dove-tailed at the corners. Standing twenty feet by twenty feet, every bit of it, from the logs to the iron bed springs, was made locally.

The logs were said to be taken out from a high bluff on Ahmic Lake. The front door to the gaol house consisted of double, two-inch thick planks, supported by strap-iron hinges made by the local blacksmith. The 'bull pen' stretched eighteen feet in length by ten feet wide. Overhead crossbeams were ten inches by six inches and set six inches apart. To discourage prisoners from attempting an escape, windows were two feet by one foot, set in the walls of the bull pen and provided the only light and ventilation in the entire building.[16]

The gaol's four cells were located off the bull pen, each with its own four inch thick plank door complete with a huge hasp. Each cell was eight feet long by four and a half feet wide, by eight feet high. The only source of light and ventilation for the prisoner came from a six inch square hole in the door.

By the 1930s when the *Toronto Globe* reporter arrived on the scene, two of the cells were used to store the village's dynamite, a third one, by its appearance, was most likely used as a pig-sty. The last cell was filled with dried birch bark shavings, a foot deep—possibly to serve as a bed, although an iron bed was left empty in the corner. Like everything else of metal inside the jail, the bed had been made at the village forge. Hinged in the centre, it could be bent back to make more room in the cell.

The last person to use the gaol of his own accord was an old homeless Irishman by the name of Michael McGrew. Old and feeble,

McGrew was reportedly fishing from a slipper rock along the river bank, when a large fish took the bait. McGrew was unable to land the fish. Each time he went to pull it in, the fish put up a struggle and drew the Irishman inch by inch by inch down the slippery rock, until McGrew lost his footing and fell into the cold water. He contracted pneumonia and, with nowhere to go, took shelter in the gaol and later died there.[17]

Magnetawan's one and ony public gaol no long exists and there are no records as to what actually happened to it. Did it burn? Or was it simply left to fall into ruin. We will never know.

20 | Lumberjacks

Cash poor and land rich. During the days of early settlement, money always seemed to be in short supply and, as ingenious as some of the pioneers may have been, they needed money to pay for necessities they could not grow, make, or find in the bush. It is no wonder that lumber companies were welcomed with open arms by the earliest settlers as those operations provided jobs and became the source of much needed income.[1]

John and Angus Kennedy were two brothers who joined the throng of new settlers drawn to logging almost as soon as their parents arrived in the Burk's Falls area in 1879. But before sending for the rest of the family, Angus Kennedy Sr., accompanied by his eldest son John struck off to stake the family claim on lots 11 and 12 in Armour Township. Soon after John married Nellie Brimacombe and settled on land next to his father's claim. Unfortunately he was bitten by the bug and took to lumbering instead of farming, much to the dismay of his wife. He convinced his brother Angus, without much difficulty, to join him and the pair went to work cutting timber locally for the Burton Brothers. After all, the brothers reasoned, food could be grown on the farm, but you did need money to buy clothing and farm implements.[2]

In 1883 Angus left his brother temporarily in order to marry Margaret Willocks, a sister-in-law of Burk's Falls merchant, Robert Menzies. Although he tried his hand at farming, bush and mill work still held a powerful attraction for him, and with his brother John promoted to a walking boss, Angus returned to logging. Following many years of working as both a river driver and lumberjack, Angus was eventually skilled enough to land a job as his brother had, a walker for the Riodan Paper Mills Co. in Quebec.[3] In later years he would recall that the job lasted four years with only one short weekend off. During that time, Margaret Kennedy would often travel to Quebec in the summer months to visit her husband.

With the Riodan Paper Mills Co. taking out around 900,000 logs a year, they generated an enormous payroll. The pay master, as Angus remembered, brought the money in by train. "He (the pay master) never carried any company money," said Angus.[4] With the Riodan wages being better than in most places, the men working for the company usually found there was money left over to put in the bank. Eventually, Angus grew tired of being so far away from home and he returned to Burk's Falls in 1903 to go into partnership with James Wilson. Together they purchased Ike Wilson's livery barn, combining it with the local transfer station.

Logging was to become a way of life for many settlers who chose not to leave it as Angus had. And, although rural schools provided education up to grade eight, many young boys would quit school before they graduated to join up with a local operation to earn money. David Wesley Basso of Sundridge was only 12 when he quit school to cut trails in the lumber camp. The bottom rung job in the lumber industry in those days was clearing trails for the teams of horses dragging sawlogs from stump to skidway. From this centralized dumping ground, the logs ultimately would be loaded on sleighs for drawing to a nearby river or lake where they were then boomed by the river drivers. For every skidding team, there was a least one trailcutter, sometimes three if the logs were scattered and the terrain thick with brush and windfalls.

A good team of horses could skid logs about as fast as one cutting gang could ready them, so as a rule one team worked behind each gang. A fair-sized logging operation would usually employ ten teams and ten cutting gangs. By the late 19th century, the Almaguin region was already liberally sprinkled with farms and the logging boom was in full swing. As a result, many farmers were hired on as teamsters taking their own horses to the bush to skid logs in the fall. These men would usually finish out the winter on the sleigh haul.[5] David Wesley Basso's father had two teams working in the same logging camp where he worked as a trailcutter.

A man with a good team of horses was paid $2.50 a day. For a teenaged trail-cutter who sometimes had to wade waist-high through the deep snow, the average monthly wage was $15, compared to sawyers who earned $26.[6] David Wesley Basso was fortunate to earn 75 cents a day.[7] The disparity in wages was often smoothed over by the lumber camp food and admission to the fraternity of woodsmen. Besides clearing brush, the young Basso's other job was to carry dinner to the men out in the bush. The noon-day meal consisted of bread or large, thick soda biscuits, boiled fat pork and corn syrup. Tea was made on the spot in a tin pail hung over a small fire. It was the high life for most young men and full of adventure despite the back breaking work which lasted from sun up to sun down. In those days, lumberjacks seldom saw what the camps looked like in daylight for right after breakfast, the men would walk three to four miles through the forest to work and then stand there under the stars waiting for daybreak.

A typical lumber camp usually consisted of the cookhouse, bunkhouse, foreman's cabin, some stables and a blacksmith's shop. Naturally, all the buildings were constructed out of rough logs. After the day's work was done, the teams would be walked back to the camp by the teamsters and bedded down for the night. Only after taking care of the horses would the men then sit down for supper. In the larger logging camps, a 'bull' cook took care of the meals. The bunk house was lit by oil lamps and in the middle of the floor stood a huge stove. After supper, the workers would fall into a regular routine of sitting around in the bunkhouse, smoking, sometimes listening to one of the others read a week-old newspaper by the light of the lantern. It was the only available entertainment except for the harmonica and, no matter where the lumber camp, there was at least one man in the company who could play the mouth organ.

Poles installed above the stove, provided the spot where the loggers hung up their wet socks and insoles to dry. By the middle of the night, the stench from the steaming socks, dangling over a stove glowing white from the heat of burning hardwood knots, could be almost stifling. It was not unusual for a lumberjack to wake up with eyes smarting from the impact of the acrid air generated by the drying. While he sat there cursing those wretched socks, all around him in their double-decker bunks, his companions would be asleep, "clad in their sweaty, long-handled underwear, shaking the rafters of the roof with their thunderous chorus of snores."[8]

While the lumberjack toiled deep within the confines of the virgin forests, the real heros in the business were the river drivers. For most observers, it seemed a strange, romantic life that these men led, almost always on the water. Since they followed closely behind the logs as the large booms made their way down-

Farmers employed by the big logging companies regularly brought their own teams of horses to haul logs.

stream, their floating campsites were called 'cabooses.'[9] And what majestic palaces they were! Large rafts adorned by roughly built sheds which contained a great wholesale stock of coarse provisions. Chunks of ham would be stacked up in one corner, chests of tea, sacks of potatoes and flour in another. And, just as in a typical lumber camp bunkhouse, the river drivers both ate and slept inside the sheds. The whole front end of the 'caboose' opened up to a sizable deck where the straw mattresses, on which the men slept, were aired.

Indeed, the river drivers were the envy of all, their gypsy existence viewed as a colourful way of life although coarse and rough. But there was no mistake about it, driving the logs to a saw mill was one of the most dangerous jobs around. The river drivers had to be experts in disentangling the logs from shore, or if there was a jam, scrambling on the timbers and freeing them up with the use of long poles. There were many courageous men who earned the title of 'hero' for plucking an unlucky comrade from the midst of swirling logs. Surprisingly, there were those hired who couldn't swim a stroke and "almost always, some mother's son lost his life and slept in a lonely grave along the river's bank."[10]

Spring break for the river driver was the interval between thaws which melted log-hauling roads in the woods and the break-up

of lake and river ice which loosened the logs for the annual drive. While the sober, industrious lot would pocket their 'time,' trudge back to the head office for their money before returning to the homestead, the majority went looking for some excitement.[11] The river drivers frequently would pitch their canvas tents on a suitable spot along the river bank before heading for the closest town. Many a wooden sidewalk became deeply scarred from the sharp cleats in the soles of the river drivers' boots.

Although admired for their nomadic lifestyle, their coarse nature was entirely another matter and those semi-annual visits to town created nothing but anxiety for the inhabitants. English artist and Salvationist, Ada Florence Kinton, who had been staying with relatives in Huntsville during the spring of 1883, witnessed first hand the disparity between the river drivers and their temporary hosts. Kinton was to spend four months in the Huntsville area, producing watercolour sketches of the little villages, while staying at the home of her brother Edward and his wife, another brother 'Mackie,' two nephews, Walter and Frank and niece Florence. Burk's Falls was included in her itinerary and the day she decided to travel north, Kinton was accompanied by 'Mackie.'[12]

Her first glimpse of the village was one of slanting roofs and wide verandahs and her experiences were memorable enough to be included in her diary. "The dogs came out to welcome us and the mail stage pulled up at the wooden platform before the large—civilized looking hotel on the hill."[13] The following day as her brother conducted his business affairs, Florence occupied her time by observing the activities of the village through her hotel room window. The river drivers? Her opinion was less than complimentary. "They're a fine-looking bunch of men, healthy looking, but a terribly bad lot, drinking appalling on land, and horrifying one with their talk. There have been a good many of them here at the hotel...Now they have struck their tents and have departed, caboose and all, and the only sign of this boom left is one piece of red timber lodged athwart the rapids and the holes from their spiked boots on the sawdust floor...There is another boom coming soon with about 70 men."[14]

Florence Kinton was not alone in documenting this legendary lifestyle. Some years later and further down the river at the Village of Magnetawan, the crown timber agent for Parry Sound, Duncan F. MacDonald was to write, "The town is on a drunk. Shanty men and river rats clawing around."[15]

By mid-April, the first leg of the drive would be just about over on the Magnetawan River. There would be one more short recess ahead and another excuse for celebrating when the log drive came to an end at Byng Inlet or some other shipping point on far off Georgian Bay. Then, it would start all over again as the men headed back to the lumber camps and settled into cutting pine for the winter. While the longer Magnetawan River was more suited to the year round logger, the Sequin River was just the right size for farmers. Starting with the ice breakup in the latter part of April, they could have a couple of months employment as river drivers, enough excitement to last them for awhile, and still be home for haying.[16]

Not all logging operations in Almaguin were successful and not every man who took to lumbering prospered. There was one company who, after a fair start in the fall of 1893, were in the red by the new year, even though all of its lumberjacks were experienced workers. The Turner Bros. of North Bay had taken over an old camp close to Restoule Lake that had been previously run by one Sandy Smith. The crew was hired and the foreman's job handed over to Tom Armstrong of Nipissing. Even though senior employees had to pay out of pocket expenses such as hotel accommodation and train fare back to North Bay, the company's debts grew. The only workers who were fortunate enough to be paid were the scalers. For some reason, these men inquired about advance payments just before Christmas and, as the accounts were far ahead of the log scale, they got their pay and then pulled out.[17]

There were tell tale signs of trouble everywhere that season. Rumours floated around that the Turners had only two pairs of logging tongs for five skidding gangs. Crudely made of heavy flat iron, the tongs used in the operation looked as if they had been fashioned out of two inch shoeing hammered to the desired shape. They were not the most dependable either. Despite their condition, the teamster that managed to get hold of them was always careful to hide them at night. On one occasion after receiving a letter advising him to return to Nipissing immediately, Tom Martin, a teamster for Turners', hid his tongs for safe keeping until his return. The skidding gangs falling even farther behind in production....[18]

Although now fully recovered from the vast clear-cutting of the last century, logging continues to this dy in Almaguin on a vastly reduced scale. Most are family operations with only a few large-scale companies negotiating agreements with owners of private woodlots.

21 | The Sawmill Was Here First

Town planning was relatively simple in the old days. Wherever there was a river with a water fall, that's where one usually found a thriving village. In fact, much of the early history of white settlement in the Almaguin area is woven around this vital water power. For the most part, the sawmill was the life link of the local economy. Communities such as Powassan, Trout Creek and Burk's Falls, are the earliest examples of how the environment was to play a key role in the survival of early settlement. Their beginnings are quite similar to one another. Here we see how one particular sawmill on the Trout Creek helped push a fledgling settlement into an actual town.

The Englishman, George Trussler, has been credited as the first man to see the great possibilities for a mill in the community that eventually was renamed after the creek that ran through it. Up until that time, the settlement had been called Barkerton. Unfortunately, no records have remained to explain the origins of this name.[1] After immigrating from Sussex England to Upper Canada's Waterloo County in 1832, George Trussler joined the Waterloo Hunt Club which, by happy coincidence, was to bring him into the north country. These club members hunted vension and their camp was located along the South River Flats, west of the Trout Creek settlement. A sawyer by profession, Trussler took a keen interest in what had happened to the landscape around him while on these regular hunting excursions. Along the Flats, lumber baron, J.R. Booth, had been busy cutting square timber to be driven down the South River to Lake Nipissing. In those days, there was always a great deal of waste involved in the making of square timber. Hundreds of trees were felled and those with even the slightest blemish marks—black knot or butt rot, where simply left lying were they were felled. Trussler took keen note of the fact that the great fire of 1892 had burned everything but the biggest logs. This devastating forest fire had started near the Osborne Settlement,

The landmark Glen Roberts Tea Room and Story-book Village just south of Trout Creek, may fall victim to the four-laning of Highway 11, if the Ministry of Transportation cannot be convinced to change the route. Glen Roberts was a thriving community in the early days of settlement in Almaguin and its history lives on, thanks to Tom and Peggy Ludlow. The former school house in Glen Roberts became the centre piece of the Ludlow business 25 years ago. Story-book Village recently celebrated its sixth year of operation. The southbound lanes of the proposed Highway 11 reconstruction are to cut right through part of the property. (As of the spring of 1998, no final decision had been made as to the fate of this major area touist attraction.)

Opposite top: The Trout Creek Store Co., formerly Trussler Bros. General Store, was destroyed in fire in the 1950s. Photo c. 1940.

Opposite bottom: Jim Kelley with his team Duke and Dick on the Trussler Bros. logging road, just east of Trout Creek, in front of Big Rock McGillvary Creek.

THE TROUT CREEK STORE C.ii

J.H. PEDDER OF THE TROUT CREEK STORE COMPANY
RETIRING FROM BUSINESS SALE.

J-H-PEDDER—NOW GIVES III

BANK.
FDLY TRUSSLER BROS HARDWARE GROCERY AND
OFFICE CLOTHING.
ABOUT 1942
DESTROYED BY FIRE

The Trout Creek Logging Co. Heisler Locomotive, c.1915. The men: Bill Truelove, fireman; Percy Bouskill, engineer; unidentified brakeman; Simon Spreeman, blacksmith.

then swept over Trout Creek and the South River Flats, destroying just about everything in its path including the local mill owned by Bill Carr. The men of the town reportedly sat on the roof tops with pails of water, dousing the flaming embers as they showered down. If it hadn't been for the mill dam, the whole village quite possibly could have burned down.[2] Trussler reasoned that the charred fallen logs he could see around him would be grist for a new mill for at least the first four or five years of operation as they were still sound and made perfect saw logs.

Back in Waterloo Township, the Trussler homestead had been home to the six Trussler sons: Thomas, James, Albert, Gilbert, Herbert and Oscar.[3] Convincing James and Gilbert to go up to Trout Creek and purchase the remains of the saw mill property owned by Carr, George encouraged three more of his

sons to leave soon afterwards and head north. Since it wasn't possible for all of them to make a living on the farm, George desperately wanted his sons to make something out of their lives in the new country. His wish for James and Gilbert materialized as they were to run the saw mill in Trout Creek from 1892 onwards to the outbreak of WWI.

Oscar was the only son and family member to remain on the homestead as Trussler had sent his wife, the boys' mother, along on the trip north. Once there and having set up temporary lodgings in an old boarding house, Mrs. Trussler wound up as the cook for not only her sons but the rest of the crew. Bill Carr's sawmill was located just half a mile west of the settlement, where the Trout Creek dropped about 30 feet into a powerful water fall. Getting the sawmill started up again was made even easier by the fact that a wooden

Trussler Bros. Mill, Trout Creek, Water Power, c 1905. Mose Hewitt, Hartley Trussler, Frank Nich, Tommy Carr, John Swayne, Jimmy Carr, Ab Borgford (Sawyer), Warren Trussler, George Carr, Tom Carr, Ab Bibbey, Jack Galle(?).

dam had been built there by Booth's lumber company. Besides rebuilding the mill to larger proportions, and refurbishing the existing machinery, all that was left for the Trussler brothers, was the construction of a box flume to carry the water to the water wheel below the falls.[4] Thomas who was the carpenter among the brothers, built accommodations for all of them although his heart was not in the sawmill operation. He later settled two miles south of Trout Creek at Glen Roberts and took up farming.[5]

The community of Glen Roberts also owed its start to a sawmill, built by men by the name of Towner and Hess.[6] Because these mill owners also had a furniture factory in Hamilton, most of the mill stock was shipped south. Glen Roberts enjoyed a steady influx of settlers and soon a log school house was built. Laura Sharpe of Burk's Falls was employed as Glen Roberts school teacher. She certainly had her hands full, with over forty pupils streaming through the doors on the first day of classes.

While Thomas was busy farming, his brothers, Albert and Herbert worked in the family mill for a couple of years before heading out west, Albert to Wetaskiwan, Alberta and Herbert to Arrowhead, British Columbia. Gilbert and James carried on the business by themselves. During the summer months, the water supply for the old water wheel ran short, prompting the brothers to build a dam on Sausage Lake. This lake fed a tributary of Trout Creek and by damming it, a storage reservoir was created. By the time all of the salvaged pine was used up, the two Trussler brothers acquired timber limits from the government, these areas being located on the south east corner of North Himsworth Township, in Laurier Township, as well as around

Sausage, Wolf, Mud and Buck lakes.[7]

In 1905 the brothers built another mill out on Black Creek, just off the Loring Road (now Highway 522). In turn, Trussler company lumberjacks logged the area west of Ruth Lake and around the Lynett and Hagan Settlements. The Black Creek Mill was steam powered and the lumber cars, running on tracks from the mill out to the lumber yard, were pulled by a team of horses named Dan and Charlie. During the winter months, Trussler lumber was hauled out by sleigh to the railway station in Trout Creek. During the season, at one time or another, local farmers: Yerkies and Reichsteins from Commanda; Lynetts and Munros from Granite Hill; Browns, Coxes, Carrs, Schlossers, Hummels, Weilers and Ricks from Trout Creek itself all were employed on the Trussler Bros. sleigh haul.[8] Soon after, other area lumber companies began using the railway to bring their provisions and equipment to the station. At times there were as many as fifteen to twenty teams with sleigh loads in a string headed west, far beyond Loring.[9]

Before the turn of the century, Trout Creek had mushroomed into a bustling community with all the necessary businesses to ensure a healthy economy. There were three hotels, the Peterborough, the Queen's and the Carr House, as well as a butcher shop, a watchmaker, several stores, a couple of churches and a hall.[10] However, the most important mercantile business in Trout Creek was to be the 'company' store. It was to play an integral part in community life, giving the employed credit during the off-season, as well as serving as a community bank and credit union. Gilbert Trussler had bought the Sexsmith Store soon after the brothers started their lumbering operations. Renamed the Trussler Bros. General Store, 'general' covered everything from groceries, flour and feed, to clothing furniture and coffins.[11] Not just a retail outlet for Trout

The Rousseau-Nipissing Colonization Road has become a continous uninterrupted trail for cyclists and hikers from Sequin Falls to Commanda, thanks to the reconstruction of the Commanda Creek Bridge in 1996. The old colonization road is part of the 'Forgotten Trails' system in Almaguin Highlands, featured in a CTV special presentation in the Fall of 1997. The South River and Area Chamber of Commerce and 'Forgotten Trails' gave special thanks to the three area businesses that helped restore the bridge over Commanda Creek. Kneeling, Jennifer Brownlee and Jayson Newman, 'Forgotten Trails.' Standing, from left: Gail Henderson, Chamber president; Sandy McLaren and Wayne McLaren, (McLaren Bros.); Jack Ralston (Codan Construction); and Steve Leighton (Agawa Forest Products).

Creek, the mercantile business also dealt in wholesale to stores in Loring, Arnstein, Golden Valley and Commanda. Just about every general store west of Trout Creek had a cadge team on the tote-road, hauling merchandise from the Trussler Bros. business. By bringing in rail car loads of merchandise and dry goods needed by those early residents, the brothers had no difficulty in setting up the wholesale end of their business, except that they needed someone to look after it. So in 1905, a man by the name of Harry Pedder was hired as the manager. Before long, Trussler Bros. became the most reputable business in the district, thanks to Pedder.

One idea pioneered by Pedder, was distributing 'store money' to Trussler's lumber company's workers. One can view Pedder's experiment as the forerunner to paper 'Canadian Tire' money. Trussler money, was coined aluminum in $1, 25 cents, 10 cents and 5 cent denominations. Slighter larger than silver currency, they were stamped, "Good for merchandise at Trussler Bros. Merchants, Trout Creek."[12]

During the heyday of the company store, the busiest night of the year was of course, Christmas Eve when area farmers from miles around came into Trout Creek to do their Christmas shopping. Shelves were stocked with all sorts of goodies not normally bought during the rest of the year and people stuck around until it was time for Midnight Mass at Father Kelly's church. The store would be jammed packed from dusk until the church bell toiled at 11:45 p.m., when the faithful then made their way to worship, leaving the premises deserted. Only the storekeeper, Pedder, remained to lower the store's window blinds and then clean up. He stayed with Trussler Bros. General Store right up to his retirement in 1912. The business then was sold by the brothers to Bill Mogridge who ran it until the late 1940s. Tragedy struck a year or so later when a fire burned the building to the ground.

Hauling chemical wood, Trussler Bros. 1918. Hardwood, cut in 4ft lengths was used to make wood alcohol, acetate of lime and charcoal. Thousands of cords were cut and used at Trout Creek by the Dominion Wood and Chemical Gas Plant.

As far as early company stores went, the Trussler Bros. enjoyed a certain amount of success,—much as they did with their saw mill, by meeting demand with adequate supply. With their sawmill operation for instance, shingles were made by the thousands, because that is what the public demanded. However, it was all to change during the first decade of the 20th century. Now, like the old- time mills, the workers found themselves out of step as times changed. In the days when the timber was cut within a radius of about five miles and transported by water or teams of horses, the mills had to either move or shut down. Most were relocated in order to keep local economy going. The Trusslers opted to move and opened up a new mill at Black Creek. However, it was to be too little, too late. The advent of the 'horseless' carriage changed the face of the industry forever. When existing lumber camps became equipped with cars and trucks, the radius for logging was expanded up to 40 miles. All too soon it was realized that existing timber stands were inadequate and unable to regenerate fast enough in the face of an ever increasing number of lumber companies coming into the area.

In 1914, Gilbert and James decided it was time to regroup and find a new use for their old mill site in Trout Creek. They approached local council and offered to set up an electric power plant there for the town's use. The price was $9,000. It was turned down in favour of a gas powered system elsewhere. In turn, the once profitable Trussler saw mill was left to deteriorate, the dam fell to ruin, and the reservoir drained during the late 1920s. The mill itself was torn down in 1932. It seemed to be all over until 1968, when James Trussler's son, Hartley, offered the town the family property and all water rights for $1 so that it could be used as a community park. When that offer was turned down—well, it signalled the end of an era.

The old original sawmills like the Trussler Bros. are now long gone, along with most of the little communities that had hitched a ride with them. But there were a few which became well rooted in spite of themselves. As other industries replaced the role of the old mill in providing employment, these communities continue to survive to this day, although some just barely.[13] The question now left is which ones will make it into the next millennium?

22 | Powassan: A Bend in the River

When the day came that the Pacific Junction Railway had to push its survey or lose its charter, the fate of the 'little village at the chute' (river-fall or rapids over which timber's floated) was sealed. Powassan, an Ojibwa word meaning 'bend in the river', had already attracted a number of settlers. A general store had been established and the first school had opened where the present day cemetery is now situated.[1] Rivers were an ideal source of cheap power to mill logs for lumber and, when pioneer John Clark staked his claim, he immediately picked the banks of the South River for the town site. At the time no thought was given to the very real possibility that the railroad might go a different route and that, in order to survive, the town may one day have to pull up stakes and relocate.

The need for a new route became apparent all too quickly. Railroad officials soon discovered that the original survey ran through a large marsh just north of Powassan. Laying track through that stretch would not only be foolhardy, but expensive as well. There were to be no mistakes made at this late a date, the directive was simply to find the most efficient and least expensive route north. A new survey, however, was to create more problems, this time in the shape of a very big hill. Known locally as the Altson Hill on the English Line, it was this giant land mass that would seal the fate of the quiet village on the banks of the South River. Plans to run the railway line past Powassan were abandoned. The community would simply have to move 'railside', some fourteen miles east.[2]

The relocation process to Genesee Creek began in 1886 and the Village of Powassan now sat on land once owned by the Armstrong family. Upon the completion of the railway through this part of the north, the original 'little village at the chute' disappeared into distant memory.[3]

The late 1800s was to be known as the 'gay nineties' and once that spirit grabbed hold of Powassan, it became clear that the era belonged to the young. Winter fun involved organizing sleigh riding parties complete with bells and whistles. Sandwiches and cakes were boxed up and teenaged boys gathered up their fiddles, if they had them, or an autoharp or zither or harmonica and those old bush trails would fairly ring with songs and shouts throughout the season. A local joke was that this was what probably cleared the countryside of wolves and lynx by the end of the 19th century.

Although dance halls were a popular part of the times, the general store also could even be a more cheerful spot, such as the one in Powassan. At times, the hall was lit with nothing more than a miserable light provided by a rag and shanty basin of fat. Or, even worse, light provided by lamps burning half-refined Canadian coal oil that left a nasty lingering smell. These poor lighting conditions were brought on by an embargo against American John D. Rockefeller's Standard Oil Company and, according to the old-timers, the only really good thing to say about the situation—"twas nicer sparking in the dark."[4] One of those teenagers caught up in the excitement of the early days, was E.J. Lawrence, or Ted as he was called. Already an old man by the 1950s, Ted did not spend his last days alone with his memories, for there were still many

The building at 191 King Street North in Powassan was John Sampson Scarlett's last store. The Irishman became one of the best known storekeepers in the early years of settlement in the districts of Muskoka and East Parry Sound. It is believed that the building was constructed in 1891 by Englishmen Edward Topps and his brother-in-law Henry Wraight, who lived in nearby Chisholm. They offered to build it at a rate of $2 a day—or $1.50 and board. The current owners, Gary and Lori Stillar were in the process of restoring the structure to its former glory, at the time the picture was taken (summer 1997). It is now known as Stillar's Plumbing and Electric Ltd.

of his old pals around with whom to reminisce. One day while out on the streets of Powassan, Lawrence told of meeting with one of them, one day while out on the streets of Powassan. The old timer asked him if he still remembered the song, 'Just Tell Them That You Saw Me.' It was Ted's song, one of the many he had composed during the heady days of his early youth and although the tune was long forgotten, he still remembered the words. His friend's old eyes fairly shone at this vision of the past as Ted recited the words. Yes, it was good to remember.

It was during the early 1950s that Ted Lawrence began writing a series of articles on his pioneer days that appeared for a short time in the *Powassan News*. Today, his '*Recollections of a Pioneer*' remain as the most accurate records available on the early days of Powassan. And it is fortunate that he included the lyrics to his memorable song in one of the articles.

JUST TELL THEM THAT YOU SAW ME

"One evening as I did rove out all on
 a pleasant bent,
'Twas after business worries of the
 day;
I met a maid, who shrank from me,
In whom I recognized a school mate

From a village far away.
"Is that you, Madge," I said to her.
She quickly turned away;
"Don't turn away, Madge, dear, I am
    still your friend.
Next week I'm going home to see
The old friends, and I thought perhaps
A message you would like to send."

Chorus
You may tell them that you saw me,
And they will know the rest
Tell them I am looking well, you
    know;
Whisper, if you get a chance to
    mother dear and say
I love her as I did long long ago."[5]

According to his words, after saying their goodbyes, the two old friends went their separate ways. Ted's memories were strong and in him mind, he wasn't going to leave the past just yet. He indicated that at home he'd been jotting down some of the things he remembered best and now the words to that song had brought back even more pleasant childhood memories. In his writings that follow he is taking a walk in the general direction of the old railway station and thinking that as soon as he got home he needed to find his pen and record his observances.

Lawrence was a child when his family came to Powassan in the late 1880s. The following is as close a re-enactment as possible of what it must have been like in those early days. The majority of the historical data is based on the articles written by him and have been complied here in order to ensure the continuity of the story on Powassan.

"It was now 10:40 on the morning of January 16th, 1888. The temperature was 40 below zero when a mother and her children stepped down at Powassan from the service car of a mixed train carrying both passengers and freight. Upon closer look, it was young Ted and his family. Met by his father, William Lawrence who had been waiting with a horse drawn sleigh, the final leg of the journey was almost complete. Intent on settling in the new community, the Lawrence family's first stop was at W. F. Clark's.[6]"

The famous roundbuilding, or "Rotunda," that stood as a landmark on the Powassan fairgrounds for the major part of this century, was bulldozed in August 1997. Agricultural Society members were fearful of its condition, after municipal red tape let it fall into ruin. There was some speculation after its demolition, that town council might hold the Agricultural Society responsible for its actions. During its heyday in the 1920s, the top room of the roundbuilding was reserved for horse racing judges, who had a bird's eye view of the race track from its windows.

The Clarks were the community's founding family and after awhile it became a tradition for them to open their doors to all on Sundays. Arriving settlers were always warmly welcomed and their teams fed and sheltered. Ted remembered hearing about the time when a poor farmer dropped in with his team and stayed the night. In the morning as he helped himself to Clark's oats, it was while taking them from the granary to the stable, that a big ram charged him from behind—scattering man and oats just as old Clark himself appeared at the door.[7]

"His thoughts were momentarily interrupted by a conversation close by and he foolishly realized that he had nearly run into a couple who were deeply involved in a conversation with each other. Offering his apologies, he continued on with his walk. It was turning into a nice bright day and Ted decided he'd do the whole town. Pausing just for a moment, a smile crossed his face as he remembered his first spring in Powassan and that very first time he walked through town. It had been a pleasant day in May, an ordinary spring morning when he set off on foot to Smith's Hardware for two, spring-toothed harrow teeth. He was just a teenager, sent out on a errand for the harrow parts by his employer John Kennedy. Since the parts were important, he was told not to waste any time in getting back."[8]

To complete strangers and to Lawrence who was still a relative newcomer, Powassan resembled nothing more than a deserted railway construction camp. Mud was everywhere. Either that, or dust. The clouds of flies and mosquitoes were sometimes just unbearable, to say nothing of the pungent stench of animal manure, rooting hogs and backyard privies. Powassan was where stores stood with their shelves empty. The two lone hotels, the Queen's run by Fawcett and the Lower House operated by Jack Robinson, seemed to be waiting patiently to see who could last the longest in business.[9] There was also a post office housed in one of the stores, and blacksmith shop. Completing the picture, were three small churches set far apart from one another, seemingly in distrust of each other.[10]

When the Lawrence family came to Powassan, there were as many oxen as horses on the street, with dozens of men throughout the day drawing tan bark into town at $2.50 a cord.[11] Since the 15th Sideroad was nothing but ruts and mud, Ted used the tracks for his mile long walk to Smith's. There were always tramps going up and down the railroad and Ted remembered that during his first summer here, on one particular day, a number of them stole a couple of kegs of beer from the station. Hartley Richardson, the station agent, immediately formed a posse to go after the men and arrest them. It had been a very hot day and the tramps had carried the beer to a nice shady nook south of the village. Just when the posse caught up to them, the men were in the process of tapping the kegs. As the beer was warm and well shaken up, when they knocked the bung—it spouted sky high. Needless to say, there was no beer left after this and the tramps were jailed for thirty days.[12]

A shanty owned by a Mr. Riley, was the first building on his right. Without breaking his stride, Lawrence thought to himself, "under the current circumstances, it was 'no life of Riley' for anyone in Powassan." Next, and to the left, was the home of James Storie Sr. Two of his sons, Arthur and Tom, were outside and waved.

"He waved back. A little further on, he noticed a hole in the wire fence separating the tracks from the village. It appeared to have been made by a forked stick holding two wires apart. Solid bush lined one side of the railway, stumps and logs the other. Ted finally came to three buildings, all bearing the Sweezey label, the one to the left appeared empty and, of the two to the right, only one was occupied and declared itself to be the Calabogie House. It was at this point that he turned onto another muddy street which led to the railway station. Powassan's station agent was on call twenty-four hours a day for a wage of $35 a month."[13]

Near the station was a store owned by John Duncan which also housed the community's post office run by his wife, the former Mrs. Chivers and her children, Willie and Dave. Not too far away was an empty building which had been used by the railroad engineers until just recently. His walk along the road, picking out the shortest stretch of mud and ruts as possible, took him to the tinsmith shop owned by Bob Inglis. Lawrence recalled, "It hadn't been all that long after his family had arrived that Inglis bought one of the corner lots at the main intersection of town. Of course, this was Armstrong land and Inglis made it known that he had purchased the property directly from Christopher Armstrong himself. The store Inglis put up carried a fair line of delft earthenware and glassware and some light hardware to supplement his tinsmithing business. No community up to that time was complete without its tinsmith. For that very reason, the tin had to be shipped in bulk and made up where it was to be used. He already knew that Powassan, Trout Creek and Nipissing, each had its artisan. The Sloman brothers were at Nipissing and Trout Creek, and of course Inglis at Powassan. It made Bob Inglis rather an important man in the community."[14]

Further on past the tinsmith shop and on the right, were a couple of empty shanties that had quite an interesting history. Ted had picked up on the story shortly after the family had settled into their new home. Like everyone else in town, he was to learn that these ramshackle buildings had made up the first home of the Armstrong family. Quite a contrast to the grand house where Christopher Armstrong Sr. lived in now. Standing in front of the shanties he recalled being told that they also had been occupied for a short time by some railroad labourers after the Armstrongs first moved out. However, the most interesting part of the building's history involved the scandalous dealings of the third set of occupants. Tenants with whom Ted Lawrence himself had the misfortune of doing business. It was here in the old Armstrong shanties, that Powassan had its first photographer set up shop, a man who also professed he knew how to do watch-repairs. The family called themselves the Williamsons.[15]

The wind was still brisk and Ted pulled at his collar even tighter. He realized that he was now standing in front of St. Mary's Anglican Church at 120 Mill Street East. The church building occupied the site of those Armstrong shanties and that most enterprising business venture. Adjusting his coat against the wind, he remembered that he still had in his possession a photograph taken by Williamson, as well as the memory of a valuable time-piece ruined by the old man A watchmaker indeed! All Williamson had done was extract the jewels from his first watch, a 15 jewel Waltham—it never worked again. It wasn't long before Williamson's shady work caught up with him and Powassan woke up one morning to find the family had moved away in the middle of the night. As Lawrence recalled, the general concensus was, it was worth the loss of a important business to be rid of the likes of the Williamsons—or, whoever they were.[16]

"Continuing his walk back in time, Ted Lawrence came across one more store on Mill Street, also sitting empty. Once owned by Tom Gorman, in 1889 this building served as the temporary home of the Crown Lands Office while it was being relocated from Nipissing Village to Powassan. John Scarlett, who was the Crown Lands Agent, kept a small stock of general merchandise on the side. Mitchell's house and sawmill business which went by the name of Mitchell and McRae, were also along this stretch of road.[17] Close by was the Roman Catholic Church and the adjacent priest's residence. Occupying the house for a short while were the two Bloem brothers, both of them priests. Also along this stretch of road was a hotel with stables. Tony Jacques and James McFaul ran the livery, with O. Shaughnessy as the harness maker and barber. Haircuts were fifteen cents while shaves were ten cents. When one went to get a hair cut, Shaughnessy would wash his hands with coal oil first before cutting the hair to save on hair tonic.[18]

The blacksmith shop, also located along this road, was owned and operated by Tom Inglis. Ted found out soon enough that it was a 'by chance' operation and that Inglis did not keep regular hours. On the other side of a partly logged fallow, between the shop and Mrs. Gracelie's Boarding House, was the office of Dr. James Porter. The Porter family also ran a large store, large compared to Milton Carr's business which was the biggest in town. Approaching the hardware store, he took inventory of the local businesses and felt that Powassan had its fair share. The community had a tailor, Charlie Frederick; a milliner, Mrs. Grasley; two carpenters, Cox and J. Armstrong; several mill operators including Bob McNee and Whorrel; and of course the school teacher, a Mr. McFarquar.[19] Just before Smith's Hardware Store, was a combination store and residence owned by William Gibson, who also ran a small lumber operation on the side.

And there, on the other side of the hardware store, was a building Ted knew very well. This was where it all began, in the dance hall—up on the second floor."[20]

23 | Fish Tales: Not about the Ones That Got Away

Spring is a time of reawakening. For the pioneer child, it signalled the long awaited end to heavy woollen underwear, rubber boots, awkward mitts and stockings. And as soon as the ice was off the pond—well, it was fishing time. Children of all ages and sizes, lured by the smells of spring, tramped into the bush to begin their search for nice long limber poles. Later on, after scrounging around the house for strong twine for lines and split buckshot for sinkers, it was usually Mother that provided the few cents for hooks.

Bonfires and fishing in the dark went hand in hand in those early days, especially for those prized mudpouts (type of catfish) which nearly always was cooked on the bonfire. On Saturdays, if the chores were all done, children thought nothing of hiking three and four miles to a favourite fishing hole. It was no secret that the Big Chute on the South River was where the really big fish could be caught. Local creeks, such as Barretts, Buttermilk and Genesee, were also well known to fishermen who could catch upwards of fifty to sixty speckled trout in a few hours. The saying went, "if a person didn't catch 50 in an afternoon it wasn't good fishing."[1]

Unfortunately, spring also heralded in the black fly and mosquito season and, with hands slimy with fish impatiently brushing off the flies, a child soon took on the resemblance of something dragged out of the swamp. However, "as long as the fish were biting, you put up with the flies biting."[2]

One of the biggest fishing events in the Spring for children was the annual pilgrimage to the Wassie on May 24. In its heyday, the Wissa-Wassa was a busy village of about 200 people, mostly river drivers who boomed the logs in the lake and loaded them on the railway cars. The logs were then hauled from Lake Nipissing over to Lake Nosbonsing and from there floated down the Mattawa and Ottawa rivers to Booth's Mill in Ottawa. And since the motorcar hadn't made its appearance yet, there was only one way to get to the Wassie—by train.

The faithful young fishermen would wait patiently at 5:00 in the morning for the Grand Trunk's arrival. At the time, all the trains had to make a stop at the diamond where the J.R. Booth logging railroad crossed it, not far from where the CNR overpass is today. It was here that the children would scramble off with all their paraphernalia and walk down the Booth track to Wassie Falls. Here was one of the most perfect places to fish. There was a long stone pier from which one could drop a line, jutting out about 200 feet into the deep water. There were lots of pickerel here, just waiting to be caught! Around noon, a member of the fishing gang would be nominated to make the fire to fry up some of the catch—and then it was back to more fishing. As the sun began to set, the children knew it was time to pack up. After fishing all day, it was a weary gang that dragged bags of fish behind them—the road ahead appearing at least 20 miles long. Sometimes to lighten the load, part of the catch was dumped into the bush on the way to the Callander train station.[3]

Piling into the station in complete exhaustion, those who couldn't find room to lie down on the benches, lay on the floor to wait for the midnight train. If it happened to be a cold night, the ticket agent made sure there was a hot fire in the big stove. With all the bags of fish and wet people, well, it could become pretty steamy and smelly and the stench soon would become unbearable, making the arrival of the train all the more urgent. On one of the trips back from Wassie Falls, a few members of the fishing gang slept so soundly on the train, that they didn't hear the 'brakie' yell out 'Trout Creek!' It just meant they couldn't get off until the next stop and then had to drag their tired bodies all the way back.

The usual time for getting back home was around 1:30 in the morning, but this did not mean it was now bedtime. Not one body could go to sleep until the fish were put on ice—and that had to be dug out of the ice house first. Although the fishing had been fun, you could not say the same thing about cleaning them. Next day, the children had to do this job and pack the cleaned fish in ice, a miserable task because they had to be scaled instead of filleted. It was a forgone conclusion that the young fishermen didn't want to see the sight of pickerel until the next 24th of May![4]

Of course for some children, the fishing season extended right from spring into fall. Back in the 1950s, readers of the *Powassan News* were treated to eyewitness accounts of these fishing expeditions, through a series of articles by E.J. Lawrence, or Ted as he was called.

A son of a pioneer, Ted was an old man by the time he began writing down memories of his childhood. A number of the stories that appeared in the newspaper were of his own experiences, such as his account of the time he and his friend, Andy Bray, took time off doing spring chores to go fishing.

It was Andy who had made the suggestion that since it was July 1st, the two of them should take the first day of the month off. As Ted remembered the occasion, it did mean one of them had to go out at 4:00 in the morning to dig for dew worms in the hardwood bush. And he was the one that went. But, with leaves and leaf mould and old rotted logs and stumps providing the ideal shelter and food for the worms, it was only a matter of a few minutes before the bait tins were full. Since Andy figured he was a 'sometime trapper,' he, of course, had a secret potion that all trappers carried with them, called 'assaportida.' He told Ted that this was to scent the bait and so he put a few drops into each can to get well mixed while the pair ate breakfast.[5]

With hooks, lines, fly oil and lunch all packed up, according to Ted, off the two of them went to Genesee Creek. It was a well

In the old days, no matter which watering hole in Almaguin one liked to fish, the catch of the day—trout, was always in plentiful numbers. From the by-gone days of fishing at Wassie Falls and Genesse Creek in the north-end, to modern day fishing at Moose Lake in the south, Almaguin continues to remain the sportsman's paradise.

known fact that there was quite a spawning hole on the Clark property in Powassan and it was here that the boys first tried their luck. Nothing was biting, however, moving steadily along the creek, Ted recalled that the fishing seemed to improve. Every bend in the creek now appeared to have a big spawning area and the biggest worry for the boys was getting the fish lines out and the fish off the hooks before they wiggled off. At the junction of the two creeks, the pair did a rough estimate of their catch and concluded it was at least eight pounds worth of speckled beauties. Since the load was getting a bit difficult to handle Ted and Andy stopped to eat lunch and began speculating whether their catch could be sold, and how much it was likely to be worth. The thoughts of selling the fish, as Ted remembered, drove them back to fishing and both of them began filling their creels again as they went downstream. Hitting rapids and along with them some small fish, the pair were to come across more rapids that this time brought a few fair sized fish their way. Finally arriving at the flats, it was here that the biggest fish were caught by the boys. According to Ted, at the time, he was the smaller of the two, not to mention quicker, so he caught the most fish.[6]

Neither of them had planned such a long day of it nor expected such a large catch, but it was greed that had fueled them on. So it was with some regret they left the creek at Jack Wiggins' place late that afternoon and headed for John Scarlett's store. While waiting for the southbound train, Andy was the one who bought cheese and biscuits for the two to nibble. Ted remembered Scarlett smiling to himself as he watched them sitting on the stools, creels on the floor and bulging with fish. And it was Scarlett who informed them that it was his understanding that the newsboy on the train might pay upwards of 20 cents a pound for all the fish the boys had. Not wasting a minute, Ted and Andy had their catch weighed by the storekeeper—37 pounds, four oz. for Andy's and 44 pounds, nine oz. for Ted's.[7]

When the train finally rolled in, Andy got to sell his fish first. In Ted's recollection, his friend made the statement that since he was the oldest he was going first and accepted the 20 cents pound for a total of $7.05. When it finally was his turn, Ted displayed his catch to the newsboy, explaining that since it was made up of the bigger fish, he expected more money for it. At the end, the newsboy paid out 25 cents a pound for a total of $11.13. When he handed Ted $11.13, well, as Ted would later record, his friend almost cried.[8]

Reflecting back on this particular fishing trip, Ted remembered that as he was boarding the train with Andy to go home, it occurred to him that up to that point, this was the highest paid day of his young life. Not only that, the money he had been paid for one day of fishing, was almost as much as he had received at the end of three gruelling months at chores.[9]

Ted Lawrence and Andy Bray were simply doing what children have done throughout the ages—testing the waters of adulthood. 'Going fishin' is a past time that has never lost its appeal and today, children of all ages continue to enjoy the sport which has become a focal point of summertime in Almaguin.

Moose Tales: A Hunt and a Stampede

"As the old slide action Colt started to chatter, Ted knew his partner Bert had succumbed to 'buck fever' and forgotten to whistle. Running towards him, Ted was surprised to see the old moose climbing up the bank straight towards Bert...."[1]

Although no one was ever to find out about Bert's part in this whole escapade at this time, it seems that Ted could not resist the temptation, and in the 1950s, when he was already a fairly old man, E. J. Lawrence began writing a series of newspaper articles on the early pioneers who settled in the north-end of the district. Many of the stories that appeared in the *Powassan News* at that time, were of his own experiences.

Since he was just a child when his family decided to settle in Powassan in the late 1880s, his growing up in the wilderness meant he had to handle almost anything that came his way. Modern day historians are fortunate that pioneers like Ted, took a great interest in his surroundings and in later years, continued to have vivid recollections of what actually had occurred. The following, adapted from one of his stories is said to be a true account of a more memorable occasion in his life as a lumberjack.

As for fresh beef, it was seldom seen in the north-end lumber camps in the 1890's, as it took as long as two whole days for supplies to come from Powassan. The day the walking boss, Joe Thompson, and foreman, Charlie Austin, left for Ottawa, it was Charlie who told Ted that if he could 'hunt down' some venison, he would be paid five cents a pound, in addition to his wages. The prospect of fresh

meat was almost too much for Ted as he ran to find his best friend to tell him the good news. It certainly didn't take long to map out the hunt, for right the next day, he and his friend Bert found fresh tracks of a moose as they were going into the forest. The duo quickly returned back to camp for rifles and food. The camp cook, Billy Miller, wasted no time in throwing provisions together and wished them good luck in the hunt. However, the hunters soon realized they had stumbled upon a cunning animal and as Ted would later write, "That old bull sure knew his swamps, and did he lead us a chase."[2] Keeping a safe distance and following the animal in an easterly direction, the moose led them past several lakes until the hunters almost ran into another company's camps. However, with timber falling and men shouting, all at a close proximity, the moose suddenly turned north.

Already nightfall, Ted and Bert made camp and the next morning as they resumed the hunt, the sound of axes and trees falling northeast of them echoed through the deep forest, and the moose turned direction again. Now with the sun on their backs, the hunters knew they were on their way home to the general vicinity of their own camp. The pace slowed and they realized the moose must be feeding somewhere. It was when the hunters came upon a level portion of a hill where they could see far to the north and west, that they actually spotted the animal. Deciding at this point to split up, whoever got closest to the animal, was to give two sharp whistles as a signal. As Ted would recall, twenty minutes later, all hell broke loose.

For Bert, well, the excitement seemingly

unnerved him. Not only did he forget how to whistle, but how to shoot as well. As Ted came running to help his friend, he was surprised to see the old moose climbing up the bank straight towards Bert. By then the animal was about 200 yards from Ted, his back a clear mark over the gully. Deciding to take a crack at it, he tried for a shot aimed at the kidneys. It was a bit high and the moose turned as he realized his enemy was now behind him. Making a sound that was more of a grunt than a bellow, the moose disappeared for a moment hidden from sight by the dense underbrush. When Ted started to close in, he came upon the moose, looming ahead like a horse on stilts.[3]

Finding himself now less than a 100 yards away from the animal, Ted drew a bead on its head just above the nose and the moose fell flat into a spring. Turning to his friend in exasperation to find out what the heck had happened to him, Bert confessed that only one of the 14 shots he had fired had come anywhere near the moose. He also had a bandolier of cartridges that held 50 rounds and forgotten them as well in the excitement. Ted remembers pointing out to his friend, that even if he had remembered the spare cartridges, all Bert would have done was shoot up 50 more trees! To keep his friend from telling the rest of the boys what had actually happened, Bert promised to turn over his share of the money to Ted. If there were any of the lumberjacks that worked with the pair still around in the 1950s and they happened to read the *Powassan News,* well, they would have found out about the pact!

As it happened, the moose carcass was left where it fell and the hunters made for camp. It was next morning that a group from the lumber camp, with Ted and Bert leading the way, returned to skin the meat and bone it. With Billy Baxter and the company team, along with half the main road gang to cut a

trail to the kill, it was was made all the more easy to get the moose back home. Rolling the meat up to the hide, Baxter did the honours and weighed it—real, fresh meat, all 956 pounds of it.

Ted would write that he and Bert just looked at each other at that point. Almost $50! Bert's jubilation unfortunately was to be short lived, as he realized his portion was already spent as 'hush' money. Knowing full well that there was a good chance that someone would squeal on them, later on the same day, Ted, accompanied by his brother Will and a number of other Powassan boys went straight up north to the Wahanapatei. At the time, it was known as the mecca of all shantymen, as it was the depot for corned beef in barrels, shipped direct from the Union Stockyards of Chicago. Ted made sure that enough barrels were picked up for the camp to disguise the fact that fresh meat was about to be served at his camp, courtesy of Bert and himself.[4]

It was a very common occurrence in 1894, for supplies of beef to be shipped into the district and it was seldom that anyone would see honest to goodness fresh beef in the lumber camps. As Ted Lawrence was to remember, supplies reached the camp he worked in at the time through a man by the name of Anthony (Tony) Jacques who had the contract of hauling supplies from the Wahanapatei as far as Hodgins' Landing. There, Stanilaus Laferriere would transport the load by boat across the lake to his home where it remained until midday the following day. It was Billy Baxter with the company team that would then take the supplies from Laferriere's to the camp which was located in a big beaver meadow near the Fassett Lumber Corp. sawmill site at Fossmill in Chisholm Township.[5]

And at this rate, what would fresh meat really be like, by the time it reached the table in the warm September weather?

In those early days there were no beaver left in the streams and even the otter, the main enemy of fresh water fish, had been trapped out of existence in a very short time. The only noticeable wildlife left were moose.[6]

During this time, Ted Lawrence worked for a number of outfits, including one run by David Moore, who owned a timber limit extending into Ballantyne Township. For a couple of weeks, he was employed packing for some timber cruisers. During that time, Lawrence was allowed to carry a revolver and one evening as the sun was setting into a blaze of glory, he walked out onto the shore of a small lake that was entirely surrounded with muskeg.[7] As he would later write in his newspaper column for the *Powassan News*, he had been standing on the east shore and gazing across the water, when, about at the halfway point, he saw what looked like a canoe upside down. Keeping his eyes trained on it, he was startled by the sudden appearance of a head with huge horns coming up out of the water almost obliterating the sun. Streams of water cascaded from the head and body of the magnificent bull moose, making a beautiful veil for the sun's rays. For the fun of it and in hopes of making the beast stampede, Ted discharged his revolver. But did the moose do it?

Not on your life.[8] But something else did happened. The evergreen trees to the right of Lawrence began to sway and trash their branches, while sounds such as the lumberjack had never heard before or since coming out of the bush, put panic in his heart. It was almost dark and he had more than a mile left to go before reaching camp. He had no time to find out the source of the commotion among the trees so he turned tail and raced out of the bush as fast as he could.

The intrigue proved to be too much, so the next morning, Ted swung over to the lake and to his surprise, saw the aftermath of the herd of a dozen head who had taken fright after the revolver was fired. As the whole place was full of moss and slime, in the course of the stampede the roots of the trees had been trampled, bringing the tops together. No wonder there had been such a uproar![9]

The Wahanapatei exists to this day, although one seriously doubts the tiny community looks anything like what it did then. With the appearance of having been thrown against the rocks along Highway 17, this former mecca of the shantymen is today, nothing more than a collection of loosely woven frame buildings left to shudder against harsh winds.

25 | The Old Moose Trail: So the Story Goes

The Old Moose Trail was laid out by the great Indian Chief, Simon Commanda. From the point where the trail met up with the McGillivray Creek, it ran south-east crossing the 20th Sideroad near the site of the old Maple Hill School. At a spot just west of a rock cut, the path turned east to top a series of hills and travelled south-east to Surprise Lake, passing the east end of Clear Lake and west of Genesee Lake.

This trail was to be travelled by both natives and white men, armed with ambition and vision. As it transpired for many these visions were to become nothing more than ill-starred illusions.[1] Settlers were to come and go in the new land, with only a handful leaving their mark on the territory.

It was shortly after the War of 1812, that Commanda, so named by the British for his ability to 'command' his followers, decided to both conquer new territory and establish a new tribe.[2] While at home in Quebec, Commanda gathered together a few young men, his former war time companions and headed up the Ottawa River. After portaging across the divide, they found themselves at the mouth of the South River. The lake into which the river emptied, was named Nipissing by the Indians, meaning 'little water.' Adopting the name for his tribe as well, Commanda then pushed further into the new territory.

The Old Moose Trail was eventually cut and cleared by his men, as a transport route home at the end of one particular summer. Smoke signals were sent to call all the parties together. Disappointed with his failure to find a better land route back to his home territory, Commanda led his people to the moose lakes, where the animals were hunted and the carcasses hung in the trees to ripen.

Sometimes it took several men to bend one or more saplings to hold the meat and props often had to be used.[3] With the first light fall of snow, ablebodied men, their women and dog sleds travelled the length of the trail with their feast of meat to the awaiting canoes and rafts for the journey home.

Long after his death Chief Simon Commanda continues to be recognized through the legacy of his name. The popular cruise ship, the Chief Commanda II, plies the waters at Lake Nipissing during the summer months. Her port of call is the North Bay government docks. As well, on display at the Commanda Museum are short histories on Chief Commanda, his family and the exploits of his people.

Just how the idea got around that the Genesee Lake area (named after Chief Simon Commanda's sub-chief and brother-in-law Genese) would be perfect for running cattle is not exactly known, but that's what the Tindall family had in mind in 1886, when they came down the Old Moose Trail and chose the hills west of the lake, staking their claim in the new territory.[4]

The family consisted of Mrs. Tindall herself, her sons, Ed, Bill, Sam, Austen and daughter Eliza. Upon the death of his father, Sam became the head of the family. His sole ambition was to become a cattle baron in the north. It took Sam Tindall some time because of the lack of a road to either Trout Creek or Powassan, but he soon had a herd of 300 odd head of hardy cloven hoofs and a fine team of horses. Relying on a large part of his winter roughage coming from the large beaver mead-

The Commanda Museum is the last public building to survive from that community. Built in 1885 by James Arthurs, it was located on the Rosseau-Nipissing Colonization Road until the 1920s, when it was relocated half a kilometre up the road to Highway 522. The store museum is currently operated by the Gurd and Area Historical Corporation. In a state of collapse, it was rescued by Clara and Gerry Hankinson of Brampton in the late 1970s. Dawn Morris, the president of the corporation and daughter of the late Mrs. Hankinson, is carrying on her mother's dream. 'Please Save Me,' the sign reads. The Commanda Museum is in desperate need of financial support in the face of government cutbacks.

Commanda Museum curator Vivian Johnston waits for the apple cider being poured by Lori Andrews while Melissa Straus and assistant curator, Jo-Ann Sikora, look on with a watchful eye. A popular summertime tourist shop on Highway 522, the museum store carries an eclectic mix of dry goods from bygone days.

ow below the lake, Sam Tindall ran into considerable trouble when this supply was cut off by new settlers from the Chisholm area moving in and getting ahead of him with their official land claims.[5]

Brother Ed was the first member of the family to break away from the land. He took to railroading, Bill followed suit and sister Eliza wound up marrying a settler by the name of Frank Wolfe. And just as Sam thought he had everything figured out, the Algonquin Park Survey got underway in the early 1890s and his land claim in Ballantyne Township wound up as park land. With his mother now dead, his own health and spirit broken, Sam eventually sold and moved away.

Other settlers were to follow the Tindalls into the general vicinity of the Old Moose Trail including one James Barr, a bachelor uncle of the family. His claim consisted of a small clearing and log cabin at the east end of Lake Genesee, the very land that Chief Commanda used as a camping ground whenever he led his men on the hunt for their winter's supply of moose meat.[6]

James Barr's claim was, in fact, the halfway point of Old Moose Trail, and a future owner of the property, John McQuoid, his wife and son Roy, were to also fall under the spell of the place. McQuoid had different aspirations than Sam Tindall. McQuoid wanted to become the area's Strawberry King, an ambition that actually prospered. The family slaved over the land, clearing the virgin soil of its heavy covering of birch, maple, and beech. When the berries were ready for picking, it appeared as if the family and the horses did not stop for one moment to rest or sleep until the season ended. The long haul to North Bay to market the crop was over bush trails, infested with mosquitoes and flies that tormented all who dared walk the land.[7] A so-called colonization road was built in four year spasms from Trout Creek towards McQuoid's homestead, but had little effect in improving the business.

About a mile north of McQuoid's, another success story was taking place, as settler Andrew Bray prospered with his crops of red currants, strawberries and onions. But the man had another, more personal ambition outside of producing a few crops, that eventually prompted him to leave the district. The Township of Chisholm had been named after Kenneth Chisholm, M.P.P., who also happened to be the president of Chisholm Stone Quarries located at the forks of the Credit River. It was from here that the stone came from to build the impressive government buildings at Queen's Park in Toronto.[8]

Andrew Bray fully expected some day to have a town or township bearing his family name. After all, friend Henry Anderson had managed to get the local post office in Chisholm Township named after his birthplace Kells, Ireland, and J.B. Smith got the south-east bay named Callander, after his birthplace in Scotland. Bray began making his plans in 1894 to leave and stake a new claim elsewhere, and eventually sold his holdings to a company that carried on under the name of Bray Lumber Co.[9] Many believe that this was as close as Andrew Bray ever got to his highest ambitions.

His father William, along with Andrew and his brother Ted, had originally settled closer to the Genesee Valley's upper end near the 5th Sideroad. A road was eventually built between the 5th and 10th sideroads, paralleling the Old Moose Trail. Interestingly enough, the property this new road cut through belonged to the man who invented the centrifugal waterwheel.[10] The special and unique feature of this waterwheel was its one vertical shaft, which was able to deliver power to any floor of a mill or factory, using water power.

According to rumour, slick patent attorneys were to undermine him and Chris Foster, the inventor, died in a hermit's shack, almost penniless.

It has been also said that beside the Old Moose Trail where it crossed lot 10, concession 5, Andy Bennett found the large hollow tree, from which the first Orange drum was fashioned and used to lead the first Orange Parade in Powassan.

Or, so the story goes.

26 | Nipissing Village

It was boom to bust in less that thirty years for Nipissing, the first official port on Lake Nipissing. A steamboat plied the waters, linking the community to the Indian settlements along the French River as well to Sturgeon Falls. And for a decade or more, it was the biggest and busiest town in the north. In fact, Nipissing Village looked as if it was shaping up to be the most important trading centre in Lake Nipissing country...

The first actual government survey of the south shore of Lake Nipissing took place in 1858. For their headquarters, the surveyors chose a spot at the mouth of the South River, naming it Namanitagong which, roughly translated from Ojibway, meant Red Chalk River. Namanitagong was ideally situated in a valley, surrounded on the west and southwest by hardwood hills. The South River passed through the area from east to west, with the lake itself as the northern boundary. However, it would be four years after the survey was completed, before the northern portion of the District of Parry Sound was opened up for settlement at a price of 50 cents an acre. With no road in place, settlers had little choice in determining how to access the new territory to stake their claims. Most travelled along the Champlain Trail from Pembroke, Arnprior and Ottawa. One of the first to arrive in the Spring of 1864 was John Beatty. Oddly enough, it was Mrs. Beatty, the former Elizabeth McMullen and not her husband, who took an immediate interest in the native population. It was a move that not only guaranteed the safety of her family and other incoming settlers, but one from which the Beattys eventually would profit. As Elizabeth

Beatty became more fluent in the native language, she took on the responsibility of interpreter and liaison between the Indians and the government officials intent on taking the land for white settlement. As a token of gratitude, the provincial government eventually awarded her 200 acres of bush land where the village now stands.[1]

One of the earliest hand-drawn survey maps of the township to survive to this day is done by John Beatty. The map had been signed in the Village of Magnetawan on March 18, 1882 by Robert J. Pope, the provincial land surveyor at the time.[2]

The Beattys with their children, James and Nancy, may have been the first to settle in the area and their second son, Robert, the first white child to be born in the territory, but they were not alone in their quest to make a name in the new land.[3] Arriving immediately behind the Beattys were Thomas Armstrong and his brother John, who had land claims east of the settlement. On their heels were James Chapman, who developed a level farm along the river, north of both the settlement and Beatty's homestead (where the Nipissing General Store eventually stood), and the two Floyd brothers recently from Ireland. James, one of the colourful Irish brothers, had decided that his homestead would lie smack in the middle of the settlement. A neighbour of his described Floyd as a big, red faced fellow, full of his own self importance. And, when his chest swelled with this inflated sense of self, the buttons of his shirt were said to pop.[4] His brother John was reputed to be much the same, but he took a more sensible approach to the gruelling work which lay before them all. As for John

Beatty and his brother Alec, they were similar in temperament to the two Irish brothers, just more quarrelsome. A hardy lot, these early settlers overcame the most extreme conditions and considered themselves "Monarchs of all they surveyed."[5]

For a number of years, this first group of pioneers lived in virtual isolation from the rest of Ontario, their only contact with the outside world being by canoe. French fur trappers in particular, would use this same water route over the Ottawa and Mattawa rivers to Lake Nipissing and on to the French River, while lumbermen and river drivers stayed mainly in and around Mattawa. Other than that, there were no white men west of the area. And so, for the first little while until a wagon road was eventually built, the Beattys, Chapmans, Floyds and Armstrongs were content to carry flour on their backs from the neighbouring community of Powassan, where the sole grist mill was located at the chute on the South River.

Desperate for a steady influx of settlers to establish the new territory, the government realized that the only way to get them there was by building more roads. Twelve years after opening up the territory, the great colonization road from Rosseau to Lake Nipissing would become the first link between established Muskoka settlements and the northern wilderness. Eventually Namanitagong was renamed Nipissing Village and once the settlers reached the end of the road, it was from here that they spread out into twenty-one newly created townships to stake their claims. Soon afterwards, the provincial government decreed that construction on another road was to begin, this time leading from the port of Parry Sound across the wilderness to connect with the Rosseau-Nipissing Road at Commanda. This move surely would guarantee a healthy mix of settlers ready to take up the challenge in the wilderness.[6]

With access to Lake Nipissing, the village became a port town with a steamboat constructed at Chapman's Landing. A grist mill and sawmill were built at McNabb Chutes and a business section emerged with a number of stores, including a blacksmith and wagon shop. Soon Nipissing began to attract the necessary tradesmen to serve the booming economy. Unfortunately, John Beatty was to die in 1883 and was buried in the Nipissing Cemetery for which he provided the land. Now widowed, Elizabeth eventually married William Robinson, the couple continuing to live in the Beatty homestead.[7]

Then, in 1886, just 28 years after the first survey was completed, all was over. The Grand Truck Railway, in extending its line from Gravenhurst north to North Bay, bypassed the village. Now Powassan and Trout Creek became the railheads for the western settlements. This was a turning point for the area. Settlers in Loring, Golden Valley and Commanda were to have access to a railway for the first time and Trout Creek became their link to the outside world. The first actual road to be built was from Trout Creek to Commanda. Until then travellers had to rely on an Indian trail that simply could not accommodate wagons. Road construction took place the same year the railroad pushed through from the south. Merchandise, destined for the outlying communities, was now hauled over the road by wagon and mail delivery was three times a week. A year later the provincial government appointed Thomas McGowen to build a another road, this one from Arnstein out through Golden Valley, to link up with the main colonization road from the south, as well as with the one from Trout Creek. During that first summer, it took a total of three days for the wagons using the new roads to make the round trip from Trout Creek. Each wagon was capable of hauling a ton of goods during good weather, but when winter finally hit, it was quickly realized that twice as much merchandise could be hauled across the snow to the settlements, using horse drawn sleighs. Because of the distances teamsters had to cover, roadside inns soon cropped up to accommodate the weary drivers. Two popular stops were Evers' Hotel at Commanda and Moore's Half-way Place near Golden Valley.[8]

During the early years, the Ontario Lumber Company had constructed its own winter road to lumber camps at Parry Sound, Rosseau and Gravenhurst. Known as the Pickerel Hills Road, it ran southward from the depot at McConkey, connecting with both the Great North Road and Rosseau-Nipissing road at Glenilla. Thanks to the government, now both lumber companies and settlers had an actual road link to the railway.

It was a blow to the community of Nipissing that the railway took a different route and slowly but surely, the village lost its prominence and withered into a quiet little hamlet at a dead-end road.[9] However, by the turn of the century, business from lumber, bark and pulpwoods managed to keep the community going and eight public buildings still remained in Nipissing Village. These formed the core of the hamlet and included the local sawmill, a blacksmith shop, a hotel, a one room schoolhouse, a combination store and post office, a general store and two churches. Fred Baechler Sr. owned the sawmill and the general store. The store had been originally built by Angus McEachern.[10] Up until that time, Frank Sloman had been the blacksmith with his shop on River Road, but he sold out to Sebastian Eckensviller of Trout Creek. A blacksmith shop was later built right in the village itself, presumably by Eckensviller. The large frame hotel was still in the hands of John Armstrong who continued to run the establishment into the new century and on a profit. Further south on the same road was another large frame building where George Simms operated his small store and the village post office. Next to it was the Anglican log church and on a nearby back street stood the Presbyterian Church.[11]

In 1902 a young man by the name of Ernie Richardson, along with his brother Hartley, purchased Baechler's General Store, renaming it Richardson & Bros. In later years, Ernie would reminisce, "In those days, general stores were the rule and we sold everything from an needle to an anchor."[12] Was it mere coincidence that the two young enterprising brothers found themselves in Nipissing tending to the mercantile trade—or fate? The Richardson name had been linked with the military for years and family members had seen action during the Napoleonic Wars (1814-1815). If truth be known, there wasn't a merchant among them. Ernie and Hartley themselves were grandsons of an commissioned Irish officer who immigrated to southwestern Ontario in 1832.

In the early years there were two hotels in Nipissing Village. Records indicated that one of them was owned by a William Beatty who served as councillor for several years. It is not known if this is one and the same Nipissing Hotel. Beatty later sold it to Harry Lalonde, who moved on to Powassan to operate the Windsor Hotel. The Nipissing Hotel was located on the corner of Nipissing and Front Streets and had a bar that was frequented by the mill workers.

It was only years after arriving from Ireland and settling in the Guelph area, that the young officer's life was to change forever as a result of the American Civil War. As family history records it, an English woman by the name of Lilla Llord found herself trapped in Vicksburg during what was known as the 57 day siege. No one seems to know for sure why the Union troops eventually allowed Lilla and her mother through the lines, but they did, and the Llords didn't look back until they crossed the Canadian border. One day as she was shopping in a Durham County general store, Lilla met Officer Richardson and it was love at first sight. The wedding took place shortly afterwards and the couple eventually had six children, including four sons, Hartley, Reg, Harry and Ernie and daughters, Julia and Maud. The eldest son arrived in Powassan during 1889 with the rest of the family being sent for the following year. Lilla Llord Richardson is reported to have died early in the 1890s, although there is no information on what happened to her husband.[13]

When Ernie and his brother took over the general store, It appeared to them as if business in the village was picking up. After all, the sawmill was running and there was employment as timber had to be drawn out to Powassan for shipment on the railroad. The men were spending their earnings. As fall approached Richardson & Bros. was getting orders from the lumbermen for everything from hay and potatoes to butter. At times, as business improved, the brothers kept from two to five horses on the road, hauling the goods as well as the mail in from Powassan.

It was in the second year of operation that the store ventured to order a carload of salt. Unfortunately, the ice went early that year and the snow had disappeared off the roads. Ernie and his brother had no choice but to move the salt from the rail car by wagons. The day began at 4:30 a.m. and finished at 5:30 p.m.

Richardson Bros., Nipissing

By the turn of the century, Nipissing Village had already dwindled from a port community on Lake Nipissing to a quiet hamlet. In 1902, Ernie Richardson and his brother Hartley, purchased Baechler's General Store, renaming it Richardson & Bros. There was still the need for a mercantile business, as the lumber industry was still a major employer in the area and people had money to spend.

In order to carry the maximum load, Ernie ended up walking ten and a half miles one way out to the store with the loaded wagon. While Ernie himself weighed only 145 pounds, he wound up handling 40,000 pounds of salt in the one day. It was hard work. He compared it to driving a wagon five miles down to the lake in -40 degree weather to saw ice, and then turning around, coming back and packing it all into the ice houses.[14]

Nipissing Village was not without its characters. In the early days of settlement there had been the Floyd brothers of Ireland. Now there was a new cast. William Malthy, the village carpenter and constable in Ernie Richardson's days, considered himself an important man when it came to the public affairs of the village. After all, as constable, it was his job to keep the mill boys from fighting when they got drunk. And they were drunk a lot! Another resident to leave his mark on the community was the American cavalryman, Michael Shea. It was said that Shea's wood carvings of horses were positively magnificent. Now Mike happened to be married to a woman, considered by Ernie Richardson, to be the last of her kind on earth, as she was both unclean and unsightly. Ernie figured Mike likely was drunk when he met her. The following quote reflects the prejudiced thinking of the time. "We never knew if she was a squaw, or a nigger. She and Mike would come up to the hotel and get drunk together. Then a fight would follow with Mike on the losing end," recalled Ernie.[15] However, Mike's unexpected death was to sadden the whole community. Ernie had been at Chapman's Landing one evening and spotted Mike's skiff across the river floating upside down. The horrible truth—Michael Shea had drowned. The village people gave him decent burial and Shea's wife came to the funeral dressed in a heavy coat. Everybody liked Mike. They all agreed, that he was a good worker when he was sober.

In the passing of years many residents grew up, then left, while others came along. And one hundred years after it was first settled, there were relatively few families left in Nipissing who were there at the turn of the century.[16]

Descendants who did remain included those of the Thomas Armstrong family. Thomas' son, William James was born on January 27, 1877, shortly after the family arrived. And although William was to remain in Nipissing for his entire life, taking up farming for a living, his brother Alex like others before him, eventually moved south of the border and relocated in Mesa, Arizona. William married one of the local Nipissing girls, Mary Helen Campbell, in December of 1903. Living a remarkably long life considering the harsh conditions, William James Armstrong was 97 when he passed away on February 27, 1974.[17] His wife Mary Helen predeceased him in October, 1954.

William James Armstrong was by no means the oldest citizen when he died. There are reports that one Augusta 'Granny' Busch who died the year before, was just seven weeks shy of her 102 birthday at the time of her death on December 28, 1973. Augusta Meckefske had been born on February 17, 1872 in a small unnamed German town. Her parents emigrated to Canada when she was just three and settled in Guelph. In 1879 the Meckefskes joined other settlers attracted by the prospects of cheap land and moved north to Alsace just south of Nipissing. A number of Germans would settle in the area, including the families of Joseph and Frank Busch. On September 5, 1892, Augusta Meckefske married into the Busch family of Nipissing. John and Augusta were joined in holy matrimony by Father Bloem of Powassan. She was to live and die in the house she came to as a bride—a total of 82 years. All of her 11 children were born in the matrimonial home.[18]

It is unfortunate that no records other than the newspaper report on her death, remain for posterity. Augusta Meckefske Busch lived as she died, in relative obscurity in a foreign land.

For more than one hundred years the magnificent multi-gabled frame structure known as 'Sunset Haven' has withstood the test of time, tucked away in the forest in Bethune Township along one of the many crossroads to Clam Lake. No one knows for sure the origin of the name of the inn, or when it was constructed, it was just one among the many tourist houses that dotted the Almaguin countryside in the late nineteenth century. What is known is that 'Sunset Haven' was owned by Englishman Henry 'Harry' Travis who also ran the place. The early history of the inn is a bit foggy with much of the information passed down through the generations by word-of-mouth. And unfortunately, the old-timers, familiar with the goings-on at 'Sunset Haven' in its heyday, have long passed away. Located east of Kearney, the belief has always been that the inn was just that—an inn. What else could it have been? The two storey main house is fitted with two massive chimneys rising up from the interior, poking their double-flue heads high above the gables. And 'scary,' was the term used by the late Ralph Bice in describing the original construction of 'Sunset Haven'. He'd never seen lumber so perfectly lined up. "The joints fitted so well, then again," according to Bice, "If you have the best in old country English apprentice carpenters doing the work, the best is what you'll get."[1]

What is known about the Innkeeper Harry Travis, was that he was the son of William Travis who came to the Kearney area sometime in the 1880s. In the early days, 'Sunset Haven' was surrounded by a sizable parcel of land which included a sugar bush. When the house was built, it is believed that the carpenters who worked on the imposing structure were likely paid the going rate of a dollar a day plus board. It has been assumed that the workers were more than likely acquainted with the Travis family back in the old country. Thankfully, what spared this historic building from falling into ruin was its isolation from any bustling community. In the mid twentieth century many of the stately old homes and businesses of Kearney itself fell victim to a 'modernization' craze as owners of those properties felt compelled to compete with new construction. Some bigger buildings, if not dramatically altered to achieve that modern look, were simply left to fall to ruin as the owners elected to move into brand-new buildings.

Tucked away in the forest along one of the many cross-roads to Clam Lake near Kearney, is the former stagecoach stop run by Henry Travis. While many of the grand old buildings in Kearney did not survive, the stage coach stop located on the outskirts of town did, mainly because of its location. 'Sunset Haven,' the name given to the property by its new owners who took it over during *WWII*, became a hunt camp after the war. It's still a pretty little place, full of mystery that has yet to be unlocked.

Of William Travis' children, son Harry, daughters May and Gerti, it appears that only May chose to stay on at 'Sunset Haven,' long after it ceased being an inn. William himself died shortly after it was constructed and after WWI, Harry left the inn-keeping business to buy a farm closer to Kearney, His sister Gerti married Jack Giroux of Burk's Falls. Harry's great niece, Dolores White, still makes her home in Kearney. As for May, she remained single, living at 'Sunset Haven' until her death. In the early days, Ralph Bice who knew the sisters well, became their most frequent visitor. To him, the home was as unique on the inside, as it was on the outside. As Ralph would tell it, "I was a carpenter then, and I tell you, I was jealous. The workmanship was enough to make you sick, it was so good."[2] The original, seemingly plain clapboard exterior with its finished corners appeared deceptive at first to the untrained eye. Ralph explained that it was only after a closer look that the lost art of master carpentry would be recognized—the boards line up along the surface in uniform precision. As well, multi-paned glass in the original windows were in keeping with the era, as glass was a costly item in rural areas, right up and well into the 20th century. During WWII, the inside of the building was dramatically remodelled. Ralph Bice wouldn't say by whom and during the late 1940s and 1950s, it was turned into a hunt camp, the owners remaining anonymous. Eventually 'Sunset Haven' wound up as a seasonal, private residence owned by Alan White (no relation to Dolores White).

People still stop to admire the former inn. But this time, they arrive by motor car instead of by horse and carriage. And the attraction remains. A truly magnificent piece of rural architecture to remind one that our past does indeed live on.

The Maws of Restoule

It was by chance that Toronto lawyer Henry Maw, first came to Restoule at the turn of the century. The trip was arranged for the purpose of collecting a deposition from a local resident. Just what kind of case he was working on and who the individual was that Henry Maw came looking for, remains a mystery. But as it turned out, having to take the stage coach from Powassan to Restoule was worth the inconvenience to the lawyer. Never in his wildest dreams did Henry Maw ever think he would find himself surrounded by such raw wilderness, the type that threatened to envelop both him and the coach. Henry found it simply captivating. Not wasting a moment after collecting his deposition, he hurried back home to Toronto to make plans for a family vacation in Restoule.

Born in 1860 in Elora, Ontario, Henry Wilberforce Maw was the son of the staunch Methodist Robert Maw. After Henry graduated from Osgoode Hall, he began practising

Taking a break from building the Maw cottage, Tom Smith (left) and his wife, Esther Miskimang, Elizabeth Maw, daughters Irene and Dorothy, and Henry Maw, relax by the shores of Homewood Island.

law in Toronto and eventually joined the law firm of Dewart Maw and Hudson. That fated trip to Restoule had been on behalf of the firm and his excitement over the new frontier and its possibilities, no doubt attracted the interest of the other partners. At the first available opportunity, Henry Maw gathered his family together and made the travel arrangements to Restoule. Accompanied by his wife, the former Elizabeth Jean McLean of St. Thomas, Ontario, their daughters Irene McLean (her mother giving her family name as a middle name) and Dorothy Hildegarde (according to family members, she hated the name Hildegarde and positively fumed at anyone who called her that), that first summer was spent in what is now known as Lakeside Cottage. There is some speculation over whether Henry Maw ever owned the property, or just rented it. Interestingly enough, when Restoule held its centennial in 1996, celebrations were centered around this 100 year old-plus landmark, presumably because it was one of the oldest buildings in the community.

When the government decided to sell off more land to the public, Henry Maw was waiting in line. The lawyer set out to purchase two islands at the west end of Restoule Lake, as well as a small point of land on Lake Memesagamesing. The islands selected by him were ideal for the privacy they offered. Apparently he felt it would finally give him the chance to enjoy the marvelous scenery he had fallen in love with, in complete solitude.

Henry Maw's association with H. H. Dewart, K.C., lasted many years and in time would take its toll on the lawyer. Although there is no readily available date for when

Upon his arrival to collect a deposition, Toronto lawyer, Henry Wilberforce Maw (1860-1922), fell immediately in love with the countryside around Restoule. It was the turn of the century, and conditions were primitive. When the Maw family first came up to Restoule on vacation, they camped out in tents. The small child in front of the first tent is unknown.

Dewart was appointed county crown attorney for York, Henry Maw who was a Liberal and party faithful, became not only one of the most well-known lawyers in the province's criminal court system, but also the busiest.[1] Now, above all else, he wanted peace and quiet during his time away from the office. The islands became his sanctuary.

There were actually several islands on Restoule Lake for sale. Island 'A,' or Dry Island, was the biggest. Slightly smaller at 10 acres, was Island 'B' or Green Island and next in line, was Island 'H.' Henry Maw purchased Green Island and Island 'H,' the latter on which he built the family cottage. Although he named the island Homewood (sometimes spelt Holmewood), it wasn't long before local residents started calling it Maw Island. Henry Maw's granddaughter, Elizabeth Marchant Maw-Cockeram, felt that her grandfather built the cottage on Homewood for two reasons. One was because it had an ideal cove for mooring boats and the second being the minimum of clearing required. Island 'H' had been ravaged by one of the forest fires that swept through the region near the end of the

last century. According to records, it appears that Island 'B' was the only piece of land in the Restoule area that was spared from any fire damage. The name Green Island is thought to reflect its escape from this fate.

But before any cabin was actually built, the Maws and their guests camped out in tents. A rowboat was used by the family to reach the island, although in later years when Irene and Dorothy were older, the girls opted for a canoe. With the help of a local resident by the name of Tom Smith, along with his sons, John and Robert, Henry Maw finally got the cottage built section by section beginning sometime around 1902 and 1904.[2] The first section included a front room with an impressive fireplace and softwood floors. Next came a dining room, then a small bedroom with a musician's loft above it and finally, a kitchen and pantry. Despite the more primitive living conditions, Henry Maw expected a certain amount of civility from his family, especially in young Irene and Dorothy. During one winter after the cottage was completed, he had a piano delivered to Restoule and then taken down the lake by sleigh to the cottage.[3] The girls, who took lessons and practised faithfully during the school year, were now expected to give up their entire summers and play piano for their father while they were on vacation. Irene and Dorothy grew to hate their father's piano and years later the chance to retaliate came quite unexpectedly.

At the beginning of 1922, the 62-year-old Henry Maw left the firm of Dewart Maw and Hudson, and went into partnership with Capt. Norman S. MacDonnell, under the name of Maw and MacDonnell. This turned out to be a very short-lived partnership. While taking his summer vacation that year, Henry Maw came down with what was termed at the time as acute indigestion and on the afternoon of July 6, 1922, died suddenly. His wife was at his bedside. The couple had been at the cot-

Henry Maw decided to build the family cottage, on Island H, and called it Homewood (also spelled Holmewood). He constructed it himself sometime between 1902 and 1904, with the help of Tom Smith and his sons. The cottage remains in the hands of the family, with great-grandson David Plumb and his wife Judith Diehl, the owners.

The Maw family on vacation at Restoule. The gentleman seated in front of the second tent is Edwin G. Saunders, presumably a friend of the Maws.

Another shot of the Maw family cottage. (above)

tage on Homewood Island for just one week.[4] The funeral took place the following Saturday at the Maw family residence at 91 Woodlawn Avenue West in Toronto. Henry Maw's immediate family was present, including his brother Frank C. Maw, sisters, Mrs. E.H. Damude of Port Arthur, and Louise Maw, and brothers-in-law W.A. McLean, who was the Deputy Minister of Highways at the time, and the Reverend W.J. Smith of the Bathurst Street Methodist Church in Toronto.[5]

Sometime later, there is no record as to exactly when, Irene and Dorothy returned to Homewood Island. Although their sense of loss was heightened by the surroundings that had made their father so content, it also brought back rage. Rage over the loss of numerous idyllic summers spent hammering away at the ivories. Standing before the loathsome musical instrument, the sisters got an idea! Finding an axe, Irene and Dorothy took turns in hacking Henry Maw's beloved piano to pieces. Dumping the piano's keys, wires, and numerous other inside components into Restoule Lake, the sisters decided to save a few pieces of the piano's wooden shell—to make shelves for the cottage. A reminder perhaps for the girls, that justice had finally been served. At least, that is how Elizabeth Marchant Maw-Cockeram remembered her mother Dorothy, telling the story.[6] However, despite being at odds with Henry Maw over

the piano, and what earthly purpose did it serve to play it during summer vacation, his daughters admired their father. So much so that Irene decided to follow in Henry Maw's footsteps and pursue a career in law. As her niece Elizabeth remembers, Irene eventually became one the first female lawyers in Ontario.

As for sister Dorothy, she married Alan Cockeram, who later became Lieut-Col. Cockeram and who during peacetime, took over the Irish Regiment of Toronto. In 1940, Cockeram made his political debut as Conservative M.P. for South York, only to resign the position voluntarily so that Rt. Hon. Arthur Meighen might become party leader in the House of Commons. The CCF captured the seat in a by-election, but in 1945, Col. Cockeram returned it to the Conservative fold winning by a strong majority vote.[7]

After the Second World War, the cottage on Homewood Island remained just as important as it always had and the Cockerams added one more section to it. Another dining room, this time of knotty pine, was added onto the south end, complete with a fireplace. Today, the island cottage continues to remain in the hands of the family, Henry Maw's great-grandson. The son of the late Elizabeth Marchant Maw-Cockeram, David Plumb and his wife, Judy Diehl have continued the tradition of keeping the place as a retreat.[8]

29 | The Bridge That Will Stand Forever

On Thursday, October 17, 1912, the same year in which the *Burk's Falls Arrow* office was built, the Galna Bridge in Burk's Falls was opened. Spanning the Magnetawan River above the dam, It was named in honour of John Galna who at that time was the MPP for Parry Sound District. To commemorate the auspicious occasion, an *Arrow* contributor who signed himself 'Pontifex Minimus', penned the following poem:

THE BRIDGE THAT WILL STAND FOREVER

"Once we went scrambling down the hill
    And over the railway track,
Where an old bridge swayed beneath the
    wheel
    With many an ominous crack,
Till we thought that surely horse and cart,
    Would plunge in the foaming river;
But how we behold with thankful heart
    A bridge that will stand forever.

The Romans of old, as I have been told,
    Made bridges of solid rock,
And many an age that granite mould
    Withstood the torrent's shock.
The Romans did well with their rock I grant,
    But are we not nearly as clever
Who built from a mixture of steel and sand
    A bridge that will last forever.

High over the stream in a noble span
    It sweeps from shore to shore,
And there is a path for beast and man
    As smooth as a parlor floor.
So there you may stand some autumn day,
    While your eyes the landscape range,

And the cataract thundering on its way
    Speaks only of restless change;
But steady and strong as the hills you scan,
    And mocking the flow of the river,
Behold the triumph of dauntless man
    A bridge that will stand forever."[1]

After years of neglect, the Galna Bridge was demolished on December 11, 1987. This was not the only bridge to span the Magnetawan River in Burk's Falls. During the depression, the Armstrong Bridge on Highway 11 was constructed in 1938 and named after Dr. Armstrong. The physician's father, Sheriff Armstrong, was reportedly one of the early settlers in the area.

Seven years after the Galna Bridge came down, the Welcome Centre and Heritage River Walk was officially opened on September 4, 1994. The covered footbridge leading to the Centre on Highway 520, is located just below the dam. As for the Heritage River Walk, it stretches from the racetrack on the arena grounds to the new bridge. Rich in history, the nature trail harkens back to the turn of the century when on April 15, 1901, the Magnetawan River Railway Company was formed. The company decided that a rail line should be built connecting the Burk's Falls station on the Grand Trunk railway line and the village itself. This steam-operated railway system was mainly used as a freight spur, transporting goods from the river to the railway station.

Today, the historic spur line has been enhanced to provide visitors with a scenic walking trail.

Peter Camani
A DRUID PLAYGROUND

Artist Peter Camani is a man on a mission—to turn the pioneer homestead he bought out on Midlothian Road in Ryerson Township back in 1981, into a mediaeval fantasy world. A high school art teacher at Almaguin Highlands Secondary School in South River since 1973, Camani searched the province for the right piece of property to fulfill his vision. From two-headed dragons to Lords and Ladies, screaming arches and a future primeval forest, Camani's three-dimensional work of art was featured on an 1997 episode of CBC's "On The Road Again."

Need a place to scream? Well, there is a place to go where you can scream all you want—inside a 40 foot high screaming head. Artist Peter Camani has created a monument to the common man weighing some 700 tonnes in cement. "And it doesn't have to have rhyme or reason," explained Camani, who since 1973 has been the art teacher at Almaguin Highlands Secondary School in South River.[1] Throughout history, the biggest problem facing an artist, is the fear of the blank page, the fear of not accomplishing. But with trowel in hand, for the past eight years, Camani has single-handedly set his fantasies in cement on a former farm located in Almaguin Highlands. He is a man on a quest, he noted, "I am a completing a dream on how I look at the human race." The artist continues, "Of course, some think it's just plain weird."[2] The screaming head alone is forty feet high with an additional fourteen feet into the ground.

Camani first came across the 310 acre property on Midlothian Road in Ryerson Township in 1981. He already had an idea of what sort of landscape would fit his dream and continued to search for it until he found it. However, after acquiring the land, he didn't have any money to start his Druid fantasyland until 1989. The two-headed dragon on the main farmhouse chimney came first. Constructing the being's frame out of iron and steel and then covering it with cement meant that the creature has become the anchor to his work. The 80 tonne-plus dragon has weathered the elements in not too bad a condition. Loosing just a bit of cement work off the claws of one foot in the winter of 1990, the reinforced concrete has held up—much to Camani's relief. What's more, the Midlothian dragon has brought applause from nearby residents who have been only to anxious to lend a helping hand. Happily, they accept their rather eccentric neighbour.

His fantasies use up some 500 to 600 bags of cement a year. Just why has this man decided to embark on a venture of turning the landscape into a three dimensional work of art? "I don't have to worry about selling the property, all I have to do, is spend my life doing it," said Camani. Besides, he doesn't believe in the afterlife. "I need something to do now, fill my time now."[3] Although most of the work is done by Camani himself, he does have his volunteers and tradespeople, the ones who fix his machinery and make the swords and shields of his knights; the brick layers for his fortress walls and those who lend a cement mixer or two when his break down. After all there are only two to three months of good weather for doing cement work in Almaguin. And yes, Camani visits with strangers who come by. But then, that means he will have to set up all the flood lights and work until 2 or 3 o'clock in the morning to finish the day's segment on the project at hand.

With his mother being Welsh, the artist is all too familiar with the supposed mythology steeped throughout the British Isles. Camani reasons, if the Druids didn't build Stone Henge, they certainly used it to their advantage. The primeval forest that the artist plans to create around the old farmhouse harkens back to the time when the Druids and their followers worshiped trees and offered up human sacrifices. In pursuing his dream, Camani has created a world of screaming arches, including the entity 'Kilroy,' complete with a 450 pound cast iron bathtub on its head. And yes, the artist has bathed in it, watching the world go by.

Plans now are to have the entire project finished by Halloween in the year 2000. There will be a five foot high, two foot thick castle wall around the house with towers on all four corners. Around the two principal ponds, Camani will have located some 200 screaming heads and animals in the compound. They will be seen from a vantage point on the roadway past his home. It will be a gallery of his experiences for people to interpret however they want. "I am living a life I wish to live," says Camani.[4] Then again, reflects the artist, if he completes this project, well, he'll just have to think up another one.

Sandy Coombs:
More Than Just A Municipal Politician

As the last reeve of the village of Magnetawan, to the elected position of first reeve of the newly amalgamated Township of Magnetawan, Sandy Coombs is more than just a municipal politician. Completing her studies for lay preachers, Sandy explains that one has to have pulpit experience to get into the course. She went ahead to spend the past several years filling in as a lay preacher with the United Church's three point charge of Katrine, Burk's Falls and Magnetawan. The course is held at the Powassan United Church and overseen by the United Church Presbytery of North Bay.

Back in 1992 no explanation was ever given as to why the Magnetawan councillor wanted out of municipal politics. Even if an explanation had been asked for, none was given by Sandy Coombs, who fortunately did not take long to change her mind. Over the course of the next five years, even when the going got a little tough, the Magnetawan councillor continued on, with a little help from her friends. Eventually elected as the village reeve, ironically as things would later turn out, Sandy Coombs was to make history, not once, but several times over.

The public's message on Coombs' attempted resignation was quite clear. As she put it, "Go back, or get lynched."[5] It was a signal for the Magnetawan village councillor, that her work was far from over. "It really was a short term out of office...wasn't it?"[6] Coombs would later comment. Five days after handing in her resignation from council in January of 1992, Sandy Coombs did an about face, bowing to what she termed at that time, as constituent pressure to re-think her position. The councillor expressed honest surprise to the public outcry. "I don't know why residents were so concerned about my decision...perhaps they think I listen to them...which I do...or maybe it's because I'm

a woman, I really don't know. All I really know at this point is, I've become wiser in a week."[7]

During her term as reeve of Magnetawan, public adulation of Coombs was never more evident than in the Spring of 1995, when due to its deteriorating condition, the historic Magnetawan lock system was to be closed, a decision made by the Ministry of Natural Resources (MNR). The navigation lock, situated between two dams at the end of Lake Cecebe, had been the village's biggest tourist attraction, right from its beginning in 1886, the year it was constructed. And its closure on May 9 enraged the reeve to the extent that she took matters into her own hands and staged a seven day camp-in on top of the lock.

The reeve's public protest drew more attention than was first expected. And it was not just the villagers who openly supported the municipal leader. Reports of the camp-in soon spread, with the curious driving in from a distance to see and hear about the problem first hand. A makeshift guest book was

The feisty reeve of Magnetawan, Sandy Coombs, staged a 'camp-in' on the Magnetawan lock at the beginning of June, 1995. Coombs spent seven days and nights in a tent to call attention to the condition of the system. The lock was officially shut down by the government on May 9 that same year. Pictured here are some of her supporters. From left, Denzil Kidd, Clarisse Ranger, Ruth Raaflaub, Audrey Hollard, Reeve Coombs, Leona Nicholls, Theresa Jaworski and Mildred Brandt.

In 1883 government tenders were put out for the construction of a lock system at the Village of Magnetawan. The actual lock itself was finished in 1886. Over the years, repairs and reconstruction work was done on a continual basis in order to maintain the system. But a hundred and nineteen years after it was first completed, the provincial government shut down the system completely for safety reasons. Strong lobbying efforts on the part of the village reeve, Sandy Coombs, brought about a change and construction on a brand-new lock was begun when the new Tory government came to power. The lock was in operation by the 1998 boating season.

signed by more than 300 people. Sandy Coombs figured that number may have added up to about half the number of people who actually stopped by to cheer her on. The camp-in during the first week of June turned into a community affair, with the municipal clerk, Sharon Sohm, lending the tent and the reeve's cousins providing the screened dining tent. This being the height of bug season, Coombs admitted to being 'eaten alive' before her cousins came to the rescue. As it turned out, sleeping on the dock at the top of the lock wasn't to be all that uncomfortable—the reeve was even provided with a mattress! In fact, community support ensured that the reeve's protest was not only done in style, but in almost absolute comfort.[8]

It soon became apparent to all concerned, that the boat lock was not just a tourist attraction, but a vital part of the area's economy. The reeve's strong lobbying efforts backed by the community, eventually brought a written guarantee from Parry Sound M.P.P. Ernie Eves, that should the Tories form the next provincial government, action would be taken to repair and reopen the lock system. The Spring election was a Conservative victory and on the night of June 8, 1995, Sandy Coombs crawled into her sleeping bag for the last time.

Unfortunately, the road to the reopening of the Magnetawan lock was not without its detours, as the face of local politics changed forever in 1997—due in part to the same government that had given its promise to have the navigation lock repaired. 'Restructuring,' 'downloading,' were the Tory buzz words for the late 1990s and they laid the groundwork for the amalgamation of the Village of Magnetawan with is neighbouring municipalities of Chapman Township and the unorganized Township of Croft. In the municipal election held on November 10, 1997, Sandy Coombs successfully challenged the highly respected reeve of Chapman Township, Sam Dunnett, to become the first reeve of the new Township of Magnetawan. It was a hard fought election that, for awhile, had the voters fearing that ongoing controversy over the opening of the Magnetawan lock would prove to be Coombs' undoing.

The decision by Reeve Coombs and her village council to hold a grand opening of the Magnetawan locks, just days before the election, was seen as a political ploy to garner votes. It even raised the ire of the local business association, although its' president, Ken Turner had made it clear that the organization did not have a political axe to grind. The president felt that since it was the biggest construction project the village had seen in years, a gala affair was more appropriate, perhaps sometime in the spring when more people, such as cottagers who used the system, would be around.

Just why did Coombs want an official opening of the lock on November 8—before the project was even completed? It was a simple decision really. The system was supposed to be operational by September. Village council had discussed plans for a grand re-opening for nearly half a year, basing it on a September date. However, after a couple of extensions granted to the construction company, the completion date remained undetermined. Coombs always stressed the point that the lock was not an election issue, it was just the way things happened. The navigation lock had played a major historic role in the community, and the last village council headed by Coombs, was now going to be part of that same history. "Of my council members, Alice Cain is the only one running for re-election. Bruce Campbell, who has been on council for 12 years, is not running, Doris Langford is not running and Ken Monahan has retired."[9]

Sandy Coombs was firm that it had been an unanimous council decision, and her council deserved to preside over the opening. "After all, we (council) were handed it (lock reconstruction), we will open it. And that is the last word from a village reeve."[10]

The official opening took place as scheduled on the afternoon of November 8, 1997, with a little help from those friends of hers, who now numbered in the hundreds. As fate would have it, two days later, Sandy Coombs became the last village reeve and the first reeve of the Township of Magnetawan.

The story doesn't end here. In the beginning of April, just a few months after winning at the polls, Sandy Coombs made the tough decision to resign from municipal council, citing poor health as one of the reasons why she was stepping down. Her resignation stunned the community, as a municipal by-election for the Township of Magnetawan was just months away. The by-election in June, would bring the Township of Croft officially into the fold as part of the provincial government's plan to eliminate unorganized townships. Alice Cain, the deputy reeve, became reeve when Sandy Coombs resigned. The former reeve cited 'unnecessary stress,' poor health and her continued interest in the lay ministry as what motivated her to leave public office. With close to ten years in the public eye, Sandy Coombs has left a pair of shoes that are going to be very tough to fill.

Doug Mackey:
A Champion of Rural Life

If it's worth doing, it's worth overdoing. That's just about the best way to describe the new Reeve of Chisholm Township. In less than ten years as a permanent resident of the municipality east of Powassan, Doug Mackey has worked hard to improve the quality of rural life in his community. In fact, Mackey has become so involved in the lifelines of the township, he's even gone 'back to the future' to explore and produce a fascinating video and enable the publication of a book on one of the early 20th century lumbering giants in

Elected as Reeve of Chisholm Township in the November 1997 fall municipal election, Doug Mackey has not sat still since permanently settling in the community east of Powassan, some twelve years ago. Previous to this, the Mackeys were cottagers for approximately fifteen years in one of the most remote corners of Almaguin Highlands. Not only the mastermind of 'Rural Watch,' a tailor-made Neighbourhood Watch program for the 'back forty,' Mackey and his son Paul, have carried out extensive research on early 20th century history of Chisholm—including the Fassett Lumber Corporation operation at Fossmill.

Chisholm Township—the Fassett Lumber Corporation. A family affair, Mackey explains he couldn't have done it without his sons, Clarke, and Paul.

Doug Mackey, his wife Eleanor and their five children were cottagers and landowners in the township for fifteen years before buying a permanent residence. During his first stint in municipal politics in the early 1990s as a township councillor, Mackey sat on a number of local committees including roads, recreation, community policing, library board and the Casselholme board (the latter representing four townships). Although giving equal time and attention to the issues explored by the various committees, there are a few that stand out, in particular the issue of community policing.

Thanks to Mackey's perseverance as chair of the Chisholm Township Community Policing Committee (CPC) in 1997, a brand-new type of Neighbourhood Watch program, addressing the concerns of the rural resident, was developed by the committee members. Called Rural Watch, the principle is simple. Chisholm Township was divided into Watch Zones with an area representative in each. The representatives were to concentrate on the identification of possible crime, preventative measures and education of the public-at-large. Once the trial period is completed sometime in 1998 and all the bugs ironed out, Rural Watch will be made available to other rural communities in the province interested in setting up their own crime prevention initiatives. The program has the full support of the North Bay detachment of the Ontario Provincial Police.

And, while most of Ontario has had the 911 emergency system in place for sometime, by 1997 it was not yet fully implemented in Almaguin Highlands. To speed things along, Mackey chaired the Chisholm municipal addressing/911 committee and was the co-chair of the North-Eastern Region 911 implementation committee. The number 911 became a reality in 1998, not just in Chisholm Township, but all of the north-end of Almaguin. This system was in operation in south Almaguin in September, 1997, largely due in part to the work of a separate committee that had a head start on Chisholm Township's group.

Mackey has always had an interest in the history of the area and finally decided it was time to do some writing about it. While in the role of curator of the Mattawa Museum in the late 1980s, he developed an understanding of the importance of logging in the area. "What happened in Fossmill and Kiosk is generic. The same things happened in other mills and lumber operations," said Mackey.[11] A logging community located east of Powassan in

Chisholm Township, Fossmill was a former company town of the Fassett Lumber Corporation of Quebec. Kiosk, located in Algonquin Park south of Mattawa, had its career as a company lumber town owned by the Staniforth Lumber Company, come to a fiery end in 1973.

What materialized out of Mackey's initial book research was quite by accident. One of the individuals being interviewed by the Mackeys for the project, mentioned an old film he had stored in his basement. He'd never seen it, not owning a projector, but sensed it might be of some value to the project. Still in the can and in mint condition, it turned out to be rare promotional film footage the Fassett Lumber Corporation had put out in the 1930s. The film, owned by Donald Staniforth, son of Sydney J. Staniforth who ran the lumber company in Kiosk, documented the Fassett Lumber Company's operations inside Algonquin Park and at Fossmill. What resulted from the find was a video, "Logging By Rail in Algonquin Park," based on the footage and produced in 1997 by Clarke at Queen's University in Kingston. The location of this treasure temporarily put the book project on hold.

Logging operations in Ontario at the time were anything but backwoods industries. The Fassett Lumber Corporation, with its extensive timber tracts in Algonquin Park, was, in fact, the largest operation during the 1920s. Originally based near Hull, Quebec, the company, after depleting all its wood supply there by 1924, moved to Fossmill. That operation lasted until 1934 when the mill was destroyed by fire.

The original film told the complete story of the cutting and hauling of trees by the men, horses and the Fossmill railroad, as well as the mill operation from the hot pond to the shipping of the lumber. Rare historic images of workers leaving the cookhouse, hauling logs by horses, trucks, tractors and Shay logging locomotives, the operation of Barnhart log loaders and the sawmill with its enormous stacks of logs and lumber, all are intermingled with still photos. The Mackeys, lead by their patriarch Doug, has produced one of the most complete stories on video, of the harvesting of trees in Chisholm Township and the northern reaches of Algonquin Park. Predictably, the company ran into hard times in the 1930s, with the wood yard at Fossmill and some of the worker's homes being destroyed by fire in 1931. Three years later the mill itself was destroyed and, since by then the company lacked money to rebuild, Fossmill eventually became a ghost town. A ghost town eventually reclaimed by that same forest which once fed its economy.

The book put on hold while the video was being produced, is now completed and details the rise and fall of a company town. *The Fossmill Story, Life in a Railway Lumbering Village on the Edge of Algonquin Park (1924-1947)* is published by Doug's son, Paul Mackey and completes the presentation of this once thriving enterprise.

Mike McIntosh
'BEAR WITH US'

Myths about the bear have been around for centuries. And if only for the sake of their convenience, myths are happily swallowed up by the public as it spares them the annoying task of searching for truth and reason. It will take a considerable amount of time to dispel the myths on what people 'think they know' about the bear, but the son of a Huron County dairy farmer has taken the lead in educating the general population on bears and, in particular, promoting coexistence between people and bears. In an astonishingly short time Mike McIntosh has achieved world-wide recognition as a bear conflict specialist. Six

Lost, injured, displaced, orphaned or maimed by human kind, the black bear has found refuge at the 'Bear With Us' agency on the outskirts of Sprucedale since 1992. Independently founded by 39 year-old Mike McIntosh, over the past five years 58 black bears have been rehabilitated, 52 of them released back into the wild. A further 81 bears went through translocations over the same time period. In 1997, he handled 110 nuisance bear complaints and a further twelve to fifteen translocations. Here, eight-month old 'Freddie' is offered gooseberries as a treat by McIntosh. The young bear will be released when ready to resume life in the wild.

years ago in 1992, he founded 'Bear With Us' a wild bear rehabilitation centre and sanctuary on the outskirts of Sprucedale. Here, Mike McIntosh cares for displaced, injured and orphaned bears and his pursuit of his vocation can only be described as truly intense. It is no coincidence that the eighty-three acre sanctuary is also his home as well as that of the bears

in his care. During the summer months, Mike regularly lets the bears who have been staying at the sanctuary, out of their compounds for a romp. The large pond on the property is a favourite spot, although when Mike himself once got into the water with them, they got out. With a smile, he explains that in the minds of the bears, he just didn't belong in the picture, let alone in the water! And since bears like to fish, it was once asked of him if the permanent bear population fished out of the pond. "Hey, they are taught by their mothers how to do that, I don't think I could even 'fish' the way bears do, let alone show them how."[12]

One bear that is lucky to have found a home at 'Bear With Us' is a grizzly named Oso (Spanish for bear). His tale is one of the most heart-wrenching cases of animal abuse. The 12-year-old grizzly arrived at the Sprucedale sanctuary on October 2, 1997, resembling more of an orangutan—than a majestic grizzly. As the story goes, his mother had been shot and killed in Alaska, leaving the cub orphaned. Sold to a circus, the bear suffered mutilation as it matured, its front claws were removed as well as its teeth—ripped out—leaving the jaws and gums severely deformed. Subsequently sold to a zoo in Sudbury, the owners later vacated the business, leaving the grizzly to die. The animal wasn't found until almost a month later—at death's door. Winning a reprieve and after being shipped to an animal haven near Kingston, it looked as if the grizzly had found refuge until a fire at the haven sent Oso into the arms of a private resident, who began the cycle of abuse all over again for two long years. Mike McIntosh explained that the haven took the grizzly back, but concluded that it wasn't equipped to offer a permanent home. Offers came from yet another circus, and then from an individual interested in the animal's gall bladder—for $2,000 if the grizzly was dead. Enough was enough and 'Bear With Us' was contacted to determine whether the Sprucedale sanctuary was willing to accept one very tired, very ailing grizzly. It's been a very long road to a happy ending for Oso, but for the next twenty years or more, he's got a 'home, sweet home' at 'Bear With Us.'

Although the grizzly has been included in the permanent residency category, another late arrival for Mike in 1997 was expected to be released in the spring. An orphaned cub from Manitoba arrived at Pearson International Airport in Toronto on November 21, courtesy of Canadian Airlines. The province's Ministry of Natural Resources had contacted him to inquire about his possible interest in caring for the black bear, with the answer of course being "yes." At the sanctuary three days later it became evident that the cub was in trouble as it continually favoured its front right paw. The injury was a permanent one and in order to save the animal, an amputation was performed at Algonquin Animal Hospital in Huntsville. Appropriately christened Neswe—the Ojibwa word for three, the cub came home from hospital. Neswe stayed inside the McIntosh residence itself, all cosy and warm eating strawberries and eggs until fully recovered.

The summer of 1997 at 'Bear With Us' was also filled with the antics of baby Freddie—the eight month old black bear cub who stole the hearts of many visitors to the sanctuary, including that of the author and her mother. Mom incidentally, became Freddie's unofficial 'girlfriend.'

The brunt of the costs incurred by 'Bear With Us' is absorbed by Mike, although private donations have lessened the burden somewhat. Employed full-time as a general sales manager for Edmonds, a GM dealership in Huntsville, he recognizes that the automobile business has been good to him in many ways. Growing up with seven brothers and sisters on the family dairy farm outside of Wingham, Ontario, Mike began working at the local GM dealership right after high school. Through an apprenticeship program, he acquired his mechanic's licence, but by the mid 1980s relocated to Brampton and switched to the sales end of the business. At the same time he began developing the idea of opening a rehabilitation centre for wild bears, for in his heart he always knew that he belonged in the out-of-doors, side by side with nature.

As Mike puts it, his fascination with wildlife has been with him since early childhood, and over the years his collection of research material has accumulated very conflicting opinions regarding the 'genus Ursus' (bears). With a preconceived idea of what sort of property would be most suited for his bear sanctuary, it wasn't until April of 1990 that it finally all came together, and even then quite by accident. Spotting a real estate photo for acreage off Highway 518W in McMurrich Township, Mike sensed immediately that his search was over. What was it about that photograph that clinched the deal for him? "Simple," he explained. "It was that really, really long driveway and all that snow."[13]

In the two years before he was actually prepared to open 'Bear With Us', Mike volunteered his time working with Audrey Tournay of the Muskoka-based Aspen Valley Wildlife Sanctuary. Tournay also specializes, but in a limited fashion through the sanctuary's bear program, in the rehabilitation and eventual release of orphaned or displaced bears. While at Aspen Valley, Mike learned soon enough that Tournay's sanctuary often would wind up with severely injured, or permanently maimed bears that could not be released back in the wild. The situation today is no different at 'Bear With Us'. At the end of 1997, there were eighteen bears including Oso, spending the winter in Sprucedale with Mike. On Boxing Day, he accepted a severely injured three-year-old bear that he named 'Nick' into the fold. Examining the bear's injures, he concluded that the animal may have been hit by a motor vehicle. Of the 18 bears, all but four were expected to be released in the spring of 1998. The four included the grizzly, as well as Molly and Yogi, two circus bears rescued from the U.K. by Mike, and Nanibush, a declawed black bear. Mike McIntosh, now a member of the board of directors for the Aspen Valley Wildlife Sanctuary in Rosseau, oversees the bear program for Tournay's animal refuge. He also holds membership in the International Wildlife Rehabilitation Council and the International Association for Bear Research and Management (IBA).

Mike McIntosh is not alone in his concern over the survival of the bear and its rightful position within the ecosystem. Extremists aside, more and more people are beginning to realize that as city populations world-wide begin to radiate outwards into rural areas, time is running out. Although ranked as one of the top three predators in Ontario, along with the grey wolf and eastern coyote, there are actually only two species of bear native to the province. The most common is the American Black bear, or 'ursus americanus,' the other is the polar bear, or 'ursus maritimus,' found only in the most remote northern regions of the province. And five of the eight species of bear found worldwide are either already endangered or extremely vulnerable. Black bears, although powerful as individuals, are delicate as a species. They have the lowest reproduction rate of any land mammal on the continent. In Ontario, black bears do not begin having young until they are at least five to eight years old. And for bears that live in the boreal forest where food is sparse, reproduction does not occur until the animal is seven or eight. The chances of survival for these cubs are less than 50 per cent.

Wild animals are part of rural living as Dave McClatchie, the reeve of Almaguin's North Himsworth Township, once pointed out, and unless something is done soon, the bear will face a lifetime on the run in a shrinking world. Their natural environment is already under fire, systematically being destroyed to make way for communities. To this day they are stigmatized as nuisance animals—shot on sight if seen to infringe on human territory. World-wide they are hunted down not only for trophies, but butchered for the exotic meat trade as well as to supply the Asian market with traditional medicine.[14]

Polls taken over the past few years have indicated that there has been an increase in social disapproval of the bear hunt, and the

Those bears who have found a permanent home at 'Bear With Us,' include Nanibush, a two year-old black bear cub from Texas who had been declawed and sent to the Sprucedale facility. Here, Nanibush is seen playing with the young Freddie. Other bears who have found sanctuary here for the rest of their natural lives, are two ex-circus bears from the United Kingdom. Molly, from Ireland and Yogi, from England. Snatched from the clutches of certain death late last year by McIntosh, was a grizzly from Alaska named Oso (Spanish for bear). Horribly maimed by his captors, Oso was left at one point to die of starvation. Upon its arrival at Bear With Us in the fall of 1997 and looking more like an orangutan than a grizzly, Oso is expected to make a good recovery.

debate is now on for ethical hunting. No one knows for sure how many bears there are in Ontario (questimates are between 60,000 and 100,000) nor how many wind up getting killed by hunters. The Ministry of Natural Resources (MNR) may have a rough estimate on the number killed each year, between 6,500 to 7,000, but no estimate at all of the total number across the province. Also there are no accurate statistics available on the number of nuisance bears shot, those poached, or killed by vehicles. On the other hand, the World Society for the Protection of Animals (WSPA) estimates that there are 400,000 black bears in Canada, 2,000 of them in Algonquin Park. There are those that feel that until there are accurate statistics, the spring bear hunt should be stopped. In the meantime, it has become an unfortunate ritual for both Mike McIntosh and Audrey Tournay as they ready themselves each spring and fall for the onslaught of orphaned bear cubs lucky enough to be found and rescued when the annual bear hunts are finished.

Mike McIntosh is by no means anti-hunter although he is fully committed to ending the spring black bear hunt, employing a strategy of quiet diplomacy to achieve a limited goal. He prefers to gain the public's understanding and support for his cause through moderation and persuasion, rather than direct confrontation. Above all, Mike is diligent in his efforts to educate the public about the true character of bears. In 1997, he presented twenty slide and video lectures, as well as handling 159 bear calls that resulted in the translocation of thirteen bears.

'Bear With Us' Mission Statement—"To promote the understanding and respect for the bear family, a species near the top of the evolutionary scale, a species in direct niche competition with the human race."

Muriel Parker
'GRANDMA OWL'

For more than forty years, Muriel Parker of Emsdale has been the driving force behind Girl Guides of Canada in her community. As Grandma Owl of the local Brownie Pack, Muriel is a wealth of information on how the Guiding movement evolved and grew over the past fifty years in her neighbourhood. Enrollment night is always special, as new girls from the community join one of the world's most recognizable sisterhoods. Here with Grandma Owl in a 1993 enrollment are: Sheila Cook, Crystal Bouillon and Samantha Ulrick.

In 1996 the 1st Emsdale Brownies may have celebrated its golden anniversary, but longevity was not its claim to local fame. That honour belongs to the pack's renown leader, Muriel Parker. During her forty-four year involvement with Girl Guides of Canada and the 1st Emsdale Brownies, more than 400 of Perry Township's pre-teens have been in her care. Muriel, who takes absolute delight in being the pack's honourary Grandma Owl, has become a wealth of information on how the Guiding movement evolved in community over the years. Nothing escaped her attention, no scrap of information ever cast aside. The memorabilia she has collected over the years fills volumes.

From newspaper clippings of Lady Baden Powell's visit to the Ontario Girl Guide Camp near Sprucedale to photographs of the first Girl Guides and Brownies from the 1940s, Muriel Parker has filed it all. What's more, she's kept those files in 'the room of no return' in her modest bungalow which she shares with husband Ron and their cat.

Muriel Parker, as anyone in the municipality will tell you, is an integral part of the community's fabric, although she was not originally from the area. She came to Emsdale after her marriage to a local boy, Ron Parker. Muriel Stollery was born on the Forest homestead (grandparents) near Campbellford, while Ron was born in Perry Township. Going to work for the railroad as a young man, Ron was not to meet Muriel until after he was discharged from the army. "He had joined up and then spent most of the time in a Montreal hospital with pneumonia and couldn't speak French," said Muriel. "Afterwards, he was shipped to live with relatives who lived near my parents (Stollerys)."[15] As Muriel recalls, Ron had to do some kind of work while he was there, so he was given the horse-drawn milk wagon to take the grain to the mill. Now, the road to the mill happened to go past Muriel's parent's home. "It was January and I swept that front porch every single day he passed by, for a whole week before he even noticed me!" laughed Muriel. Their first date? "He called up on the following Monday to see if I wanted to go to a hockey game."[16]

Muriel Parker's first visit to Emsdale was back on April 20, 1946. "That was the day of Ron's grandfather's funeral," said Muriel. "William Hart had been born in 1856. He sure lived a long time."[17] The Parkers made their move to Emsdale in 1949 and five years later, Muriel joined Girl Guides of Canada as a guider. Today, despite her years, Grandma Owl continues to play a major role in her Brownies' lives. And how things have changed over the past forty some years. Although the pack now meets on a weekly basis at the Evergreen Heights Education Centre (public school) in Emsdale, it wasn't always so. According to Muriel, in summers gone by, meetings were often held at the 'door yard' (meaning—her back yard). Camping was done inside the community centre, and not at Doe Lake. "I'd sleep in the middle of the hall where I could keep an eye open on the girls. By morning, I'd find hot little breaths all around me," recalls Muriel.[18] Later on as the pack grew, the meetings were held at either the Orange Lodge, the Perry Central Public School (Perry Central Apartments), or the basements of the local Anglican and United Churches. A permanent move was made to the Emsdale Community Centre and the meetings continued to be held there until the fall of 1997 before the move to the public school. Before the Town of Kearney ended up with its own Brownie pack in the 1970s, Kearney girls were a part of the Emsdale guiding experience. Now the 1st Emsdale Brownies draws its membership from both Perry and McMurrich townships.

When Muriel Parker signed up to be a guider with the 1st Emsdale Brownies back in

September of 1953, there were fifteen girls registered. Due to an oversight, Muriel was not registered formally as a guider until 1955. "They (District Commissioner) forgot—for two whole years!" laughed Muriel.[19] Her so-called 40th anniversary was celebrated in February of 1995 with a surprise Tea at the Emsdale Community Centre. And a surprise it was, considering she has been in charge of hall rentals for a number of years. "I was told at the time the community centre was being booked for a Thinking Day celebration," said the bemused Muriel. "It wasn't now, was it?"[20] For those not familiar with the guiding movement, Thinking Day marks the birthdays of Lord and Lady Baden Powell, founders of the Boy Scout and Girl Guide movements.

While Grandma Owl was completing the 50 year history of the 1st Emsdale Brownies in time for the golden anniversary in October of 1996, there was much for her to reflect on. Just the year before, several granddaughters of her first Brownies joined the pack, continuing the link to the past. "I've played the organ at my Brownies' weddings—for love,"[21] says Muriel. A few of those weddings that she remembers, were for Shannon Gilpin, Penny Appleyard and Kathy Arrowsmith. On a more somber note, she has also witnessed the burial of three of her Brownies, the first one being Rita Leigh, who died in a house fire. Just one of the many realities of Mrs. Muriel Parker's extraordinary career as a volunteer in Guiding, which she is continuing to this day.

31 | Gone but Not Forgotten

Hartley Trussler & Ralph Bice

Hartley Trussler (March 14, 1897 - December 13, 1990) and Ralph Bice (March 2, 1900 - August 22, 1997) were the best kind of local historians. Faithfully committing to paper the everyday activities that took place around them, no detail was too small to escape either man's attention. The end result? Lively tales of the early days in Almaguin which were read widely each week in the local newspaper. Both men became regular columnists and while Hartley Trussler's 'Reflections' first appeared in the *Burk's Falls Arrow* and *Sundridge Echo* during the 1960s, Ralph Bice started his column, 'Along The Trail' in 1970. By this time the old *Arrow,* as it was known, had been renamed the *Almaguin News* (combining the *Powassan News, Sundridge Echo* and *Burk's Falls Arrow*). Both columns appeared on a regular basis throughout the 1970s, with 'Along The Trail' becoming a regular fixture on the editorial page well into the 1990s. Ralph Bice's granddaughter, Kelly Marshall of Emsdale, who had been transcribing her grandfather's tapes for his column when his health began to fail, wrote the final installment of 'Along the Trail' for the newspaper shortly after his death.

Hartley Trussler's 'Reflections' covered a multitude of subject matters dealing with village life in the north-end of Almaguin and some of the funniest columns were based on actual incidents from his own youth. On January 21, 1976, he began his series on rural life during the years between 1900 and 1976. Among the more memorable articles was one on spring cleaning. With most families growing vegetables on the farm, after the harvest, the potatoes and turnips were kept in bins in the cellar. According to Hartley Trussler, in days gone by, cleaning up the cellar was included as part of the children's chores. By spring as he was to write, most of the vegetables stored over the winter had long sprouts and many were rotten. It was up to the children to de-sprout them and pick out the rotten ones. "Those mushy, rotten turnips and potatoes were about the messiest, stinkin' things you could imagine, but it had to be done and those kids did it."[1] Another spring ritual for the children was cleaning out the outhouse. The way Hartley Trussler described it, a pit was dug in the corner of the garden and the contents wheeled from the privy to the pit. "When you started the job you were almost overcome with nausea, but you soon got used to it. When Dad told us to do something, we never questioned it."[2]

Of course, 'Reflections' did include more adult themes. Ten years earlier, on November 2 of 1966, Hartley Trussler wrote about the old commercial travellers, the original PR men (public relations), he called them. These were the men who advertised, promoted and sold their wares and brought the city way of life to small towns and villages in Almaguin. Local hotels where they stayed became lively night spots and were soon turned into viable 'Commercial Houses.' "At night when a bunch of travellers got together, there was always great revelry and you never knew what was going to happen. They were the Dr. Jekyll and Mr. Hyde. During the days, serious business ambassadors—at night, regular devils of gaiety."[3] Hartley Trussler always suspected that many of the local hotel waitresses and chambermaids could have told some great stories—

Whose who? Young Hartley Trussler at the age of nine is pictured here (front row-marked with a star) in the class of 1906. Although there are 48 of 53 names provided for his classmates, they are in alphabetical order: Leila and Chrismans Bogford; Isobel Brown; Cora, Julia and Lois Carr; Lee, Mary, Nellie and Seth Cowden; Bob and Duff Evers; Rhea Green; James, Joe, Marg and Willis Hagen; Lillian Hainstock; James, Joe and John Hamson; Willie Hornsby; Nellie Lawrence; John B., Mary Ellen and Thomas Lynett; Angus MacDonald; John MacSwain; Edna and Hubert Mullen; Denny and Kate Nigh; Minnie and Tillie Norbon; Hazel Scriven; Kate Sloman; Mary, Nellie and Johnny Stellar; Dora and Hartley Trussler; Alberta, Joe and Rachel Whitehead; Miss Kennedy and Mr. Maxwell, Teachers.

if they'd been brave enough to do so.

Hartley Trussler, in writing 'family history' in his column, has left a priceless record of pioneer life in Almaguin. The original dam at the Trussler Bros. Mill at Trout Creek is one example. It was built by the men working for the late 19th century's greatest lumber baron, J. R. Booth. These men were also responsible for constructing the great log slides at the Chutes at Geisler, Chapman and Nipissing. J. R. Booth had timber limits in and around Lake Nipissing, up the Sturgeon River and Duchesnay Creek, as well as the South River and Trout Creek. In fact, any stream in the area which could float logs, somehow wound up belonging to Booth. And on all of them he built dams and log slides to sluice his logs and square timber over the falls and rapids. As Hartley Trussler records it, the lumber baron cut the pine off the Trout Creek and South River flats about 1889 and had them driven down to Lake Nipissing. The majority of the best quality trees were made into square timber and, in separating the best from the rest, there were hundreds chopped down and left where they were felled.

"Grandfather (George Trussler) used to come up deer hunting with Merner and a gang from Waterloo and he saw all these logs laying on the ground wasting. He thought it was the opportune time for his sons to go into the sawmill business."[4] Hartley Trussler's father and his brothers were not the only ones to benefit, for J.R. Booth's cull logs were the source of income for many entrepreneurs in those early years. There is little doubt that without lumbermen such as Booth, early settlement in Almaguin would have been minimal.

In the case of the Trusslers, J.R. Booth had laid the foundations for a great family empire which lasted well into the early part of the 20th century. Trussler Bros. logging operations, during the years between 1905 and 1909 had expanded approximately five miles northeast of Trout Creek into South Himsworth Township, along the McGillvary Creek. A road followed the creek from the top of the hill down into the low land, then out to the Grand Trunk railway line and back into the swamp and on south to the village of Trout Creek itself. The company men used this road from the railroad crossing up to the mill at the falls. A portion of the road at the top of the first sand hill was bridged over by the little stream. Hartley Trussler was to make a note of this road in one of his photo albums, as being quite a feat of road construction over very difficult terrain. He also mentioned the considerable cost incurred to build it, although no dollar figure was used.

Loggers for the Trussler Bros. utilized large, homemade sleighs with ten foot bunks which were loaded with logs until they formed a peak. One such team, Hartley Trussler recalled, had all it could draw just on the level portion of the road. Coming up the little grade from the railway to the business sec-tion of town, a tow-team was then needed to help it along. As Trussler remembered it, "This team was a big rangy span of grey percherons bought in Toronto. The teamster was Jim Keeley. I can remember him coming down the lower part of the sand hill on the dead gallop and as he passed the camp, he was waving his hat and yelling like an Indian."[5]

While Hartley Trussler concentrated on village life and its transition into modern times, Ralph stuck with what he knew best—the land itself.

In Ralph Bice's life there was only one passion, trapping. And he thoroughly enjoyed the anecdotes about how he got into the business,

Trussler Bros. Mill at Trout Creek in 1917. The original sawmill was built by Bill Carr around 1887 and destroyed in the great fire of 1892. The Trussler brothers, James and Gilbert bought the property after the fire and rebuilt the sawmill. In 1925, the mill was torn down. Hartley Trussler bought the property from his dad, James, in 1947 for $450. The site of the old sawmill was offered free of charge to the Town of Trout Creek in 1968 for use as a possible park. The offer was turned down. Hartley sold it in 1978 to Cletus Hummel for $2,500.

The Wright Brothers had not even flown the first airplane when Ralph Bice set his first trap as a young child. A true frontiersman all his life, he was what one would describe as a man's man. Rarely getting out of the woods around his home base, the Town of Kearney. Although Ralph promoted humane trapping of animals, he did not have much time for animal activists opposed to the trapping of all animals.

never tiring of repeating the stories to whomever would listen. Ralph used to tell people that reason he got such a late start as a trapper, was because his father, Fred Bice, wouldn't let him go alone in a canoe until he was four. The second version has Ralph at the age of four going along with his father into the bush alright, but where Bice Sr. did all the trapping, Ralph got to carry that canoe! Over the years Ralph Bice honed his skills to the point, that eventually it earned him the nickname 'King Trapper.' And there are many who will attest to man's talents as a trapper and first-class skinner. Ralph taught trapping, fur-handling and conservation to school-aged children from the primary grades onwards, as well as teaching the skills to other trappers across the country.

Born in West Guilford near Haliburton, Ralph was one of seven children and the only one to eventually follow in his father's and grandfather's footsteps as a full-time outdoorsman. Ralph's grandfather, Issac Bice, trapped the area that in 1893, became part of Algonquin Park and as Ralph likes to tell it, his grandfather was The Park's first poacher to

get arrested. When Fred Bice, who was a park ranger, moved his family to Kearney on the western boundary of Algonquin Park in 1911, Ralph was more than ready to head off into the bush.[6] At the age of 17, he got the break he was looking for by becoming a Park guide. He though he'd gone to heaven, getting paid to fish every day. Although Ralph spent most of his life in the bush, he did find time to write his newspaper column 'Along The Trail', along with five books. In all of them he wrote about what he knew best, living off the land. That accumulated knowledge eventually earned him a second nickname —'Old Man of Algonquin Park.'

Marrying Edna Merrifield in 1925 didn't stop Ralph from staying away for long periods of time. Edna was left to raise their seven children on her own. Their family eventually grew to include twenty-four grandchildren and forty-one great-grandchildren whose affiliation with The Park was to span six generations. Sadly, after sixty-four years of marriage, Ralph's partner-for-life died in 1989, after a lengthy illness.

Today, five of the seven Bice children continue to reside in the area: Marilyn McKay and Phyllis McKay in Kearney; Sharon Wilhelm in Emsdale; Janet Johnston in Torrance and brother Doug in Melissa. Peggy Sochasky is the only member of the immediate family who does not live in the area. The Sochaskys are in Waterloo. Ralph and Edna's eldest son, Fred, passed away in 1950.

A civic-minded individual and a devout Christian, Ralph,with the help of the local historical society, made sure a cairn was erected at Kearney's main waterfront as a tribute to the early settlers of the area. He also founded the Civic Holiday weekend Kearney Regatta that continues to this day as the oldest regatta in Almaguin. Ralph served on municipal council, both as councillor and then as mayor from 1939 to 1946, as well as being a school board trustee and lay preacher at Knox United Church in Kearney.

His greatest public honour came in October of 1985 when he was awarded the Order of Canada. And at the age of 84, Ralph Bice showed he hadn't slowed down one bit. First off, Ralph wasn't going to accept the honour unless it was simply inscribed, 'Ralph Bice, trapper.' And as a staunch Tory, he turned in his seat to another Order of Canada recipient, the former Prime Minister Pierre Trudeau, to inform him that, "He was the luckiest fellow in the room." When Trudeau asked, "Why is that?" Ralph replied, "Because there's only one old trapper here and you got to sit next to him."[7]

Ralph Bice promoted the humane trapping of animals, but he did not have much time for animal activists opposed to the trapping of all animals. Gary Ball, an outdoors writer and member of an advisory board for provincial fish and wildlife programs, first met Ralph Bice more than thirty years ago and soon learned to appreciate the trapper's stance with what Ball referred to as 'tree-huggers and armchair conservationists.' "As a print reporter, and author, I soon learned, that there was nothing that would sway Ralph from his opinions. There were many 'arguments' over the years in regards to Ralph's position on wolves—and my own. It always started the same way, and ended the same way—his feeling was that the only good wolf, was a single she-wolf to every two hundred miles. Now, how do you argue with logic like that?"[8]

Ralph Bice often remarked that when he died and happened to go to heaven, he would probably be disappointed because it would not be as nice as Algonquin Park. But although he had the makings of a great trapper, he also pursued a literary career and became the author of five books. During his senior years, Ralph took over from Hartley Trussler of Trout Creek and continued writing a newspaper column in the *Almaguin News* in Burk's Falls. Both men wrote about what they knew best—the frontier days.

For Ralph and Edna's 60th wedding anniversary, the Burk's Falls Trappers Council gave him a fur hat. We do not know what Edna got out of the deal. Ralph helped found the Ontario Trappers Association in 1947 and was the holder of one of the province's first registered trapping zones.

At Ralph Bice's funeral on August 25, 1997, at the Kearney Community Centre, retired reverend and eulogist for the service, Dorothy Wilson stated that Ralph had always been fond of the poem:

'A bell's not a bell 'till you ring it
A song's not a song 'till you sing it.'

In keeping with the sentiment of the poem, the family had requested that anyone wishing to make a donation in memory of Ralph Bice, could do so by contributing to the Kearney Knox United Church bell tower fund. At last count, that fund stood at $2,800. According his daughter, Marilyn MacKay, the tower itself was restored in the Fall and a plaque will be unveiled at the Bice family reunion on August 16, 1998. Said Marilyn, "Since Aunt Bessie (Ralph's youngest sister, age 88) has the church service for the reunion already all planned, now I've got to get her to work out what's going on that plaque!"[9]

On November 29, 1997, Ralph Bice was posthumously honoured at the 50th Anniversary of the Burk's Falls Trappers Council held in Katrine. The evening was fittingly named, 'A Tribute to a Trapper—Ralph Bice.' Not only did he help found the Ontario Trappers Association in 1947, but he founded the first trappers' council in the province at Burk's Falls. Ralph Bice became a charter member and past president of the Association (1954 - 1960) and is on record as the holder of one of the province's first registered trapping zones. Today, the traplines which sustained Ralph Bice's family through much of this century, continue to produce a fur harvest of renown quality. Since the inception of the Burk's Falls Trappers Council, a total of 98 councils have been formed, representing all trapping areas in Ontario.

The following poem, 'The Millionaire' was a personal tribute at the 50th anniversary of the Burk's Falls Trappers Council to the legendary trapper and woodsman and included in the printed program. It was submitted by a lady trapper and associate of Ralph's, Paton Lodge-Lindsay. She received her first trapper's licence in 1968 and during all those years, Paton never lost her admiration for a man who revolutionized the Ontario trapping industry, making it a model followed worldwide. From her perspective, this poem written by an anonymous poet, symbolized everything that Ralph Bice was and stood for. It was well received by those in attendance that night.

THE MILLIONAIRE

"I've got my name on the river,
I've got my name on the sea,
I've got my name on the summer skies,
They all belong to me.

I've got my name on the violets
That grow in their corner fair,
And where ever Nature has planted Peace
My name is written there.

As far as the eye can travel
From where I stand in the sun,
I've got my name on the things I see,
And I own them, every one.

I've got my name on the singing birds
That mate when spring is new,
But I won't be selfish with all these things,
I'll share them friend, with you.

There is no deed to the river.
There is no lock to the sea.
Not all the power in the world
Can take their joy from me.

There is no fence 'round' the heavens.
No vault holds the sunset's gold.
The earth is mine and the heavens are mine
'Til all of the suns grow cold.

The starts are my thousand jewels,
And Life is my bread and wine,
And all that I see was made for me
And all that I love is mine.'

Anonymous.

In 1998, the Friends of Algonquin began what they hope will be a successful lobby to have Butt Lake in Algonquin Park renamed in memory of Ralph Bice. The board of directors of the organization sent a proposal to Morgan Goadsby, the manager of the provincial Geo-referencing Centre of the Ministry of Natural Resources (MNR) for the official name change. Members of the Friends of Algonquin also launched a letter writing campaign to solicit support for the proposal. There has been no indication given, as to when the renaming of the lake is to officially take place. Throughout his guiding career, Ralph made the lake his starting point for the numerous trips into the Park, often staying in the ranger cabin built by his father. It is very clear from Ralph's own writing that this was his favourite lake. Of course, when he first came across it, it was called Eagle Lake. That memorable first visit in 1912, moved him to write, "It was late in the afternoon when we arrived at Eagle Lake, which I thought then and still think is just about the most beautiful lake, not only in Algonquin Park but in Ontario."[10]

The name Eagle Lake was adopted by the early trappers, for the eagles who nested on a cliff along the south side of the lake. However, by the early 1930s, when topographical maps were vastly improved, there was a move by the government to eliminate duplication of lake names. Since eagles no longer nested near the lake and there were other Eagle lakes, the name was changed to that of the municipality where it was located. Butt Township was surveyed in 1879 and named after Irish nationalist Isaac Butt. There is no documentation to prove that Butt, who died in Dublin that year, had ever visited Canada, or had any connection with the area that was named in his honour. According to Marilyn (Bice) MacKay of Kearney, her late father had wanted the name Eagle Lake retained, however, there are precedents for renaming lakes within Algonquin Park. Two that come to mind are Tom Thomson Lake and Carl Wilson Lake.

Epilogue

Just where did the name come from? According to a 1960s newscap in the *Burk's Falls Arrow and Sundridge Echo* (later the *Almaguin News*), the name Almaguin evolved out of a late 1950s battle for tourist dollars within the District of Parry Sound.

Members of the Magnetawan River and Lakes Tourist Association felt that the way to give local tourism a necessary boost was to create an identity to set the east side of the district apart from the rest of Parry Sound. In the summer of 1958, they set off to find a new name by running a contest in the *Burk's Falls Arrow*. Members were looking for something that would clearly define the region bounded by Huntsville, North Bay, Algonquin Park and Dunchurch, in the minds of prospective vacationers. A specific name would help tourists easily differentiate the east side from the west side when they picked out their travel destination. After all, the Town of Parry Sound, conveniently located on the shores of Georgian Bay, had anchored the district long enough. Now was the time to break away and form a new identity.

Name-The-Area-Contest offering $50 as a prize, more than 100 entries were submitted. Interestingly enough, a tourist won. Jean Sutherland, of Forest Hill in Toronto, submitted 'Almaguin—Algonquin-Magnetawan Highlands.' AL, from the word Algonquin denoted the indigenous tribe that regularly hunted in the area. MAG, stood for Magnetawan River which cuts through the heart of the highlands and UIN, pronounced WIN, supposedly was added to create an Indian flavour and tie in with the area being a communal hunting ground of the native population. "It

was a 'good old Indian name'—the same as Muskoka and Algoma—manufactured by the white man," stated the *Arrow*.

Sutherland's entry was chosen by a committee of eight area businessmen. Representing the South River Chamber of Commerce, were Ron Hall, Clarke Stevenson and Stuart Dennis. Sitting on the committee on behalf of the Sundridge Chamber of Commerce were Earl Anderson, Bill Vrooman and D. R. Kidd. Morrison, 'Morry Barr,' soon-to-be publisher of the *Almaguin News* and Harvey Raaflaub represented the tourist association.

Finally the breathtaking hills of Almaguin Highlands were open for a new era in tourism. With sparkling waterways criss-crossing the vast lakeland area, the region has everything from pristine beaches to rapids and some of the best traditional fishing grounds in the province. Covering an area that begins just north of Huntsville, visitors are warmly greeted by Novar, the Highlands first community. And along the 90 kilometre strip of Highway 11, north to Callander, are the many picturesque hamlets, villages and towns that stand today as testimonials to the white pioneers that first settled the region more than 100 years ago. But there is still more. The region in fact reaches as far out as the eastern boundary of Algonquin Park and then westward towards Georgian Bay for approximately fifty kilometres.

Almaguin Highlands continues to welcome one and all. If you are planning to escape to Ontario's great outdoors for fun and for exploration into the past—head for the hills—The Almaguin Highlands hills!

Notes

INTRODUCTION

1 *Toronto Mail,* Saturday, July 30, 1892.
2 *Ibid.*

CHAPTER 1 SETTLING THE NEW LAND

1 Ada Florence Kinton, *Just One Blue Bonnet, The Life Story of Ada Florence Kinton.* Edited by her sister, Sara A. Randleson. (Toronto, William Briggs, 1907). p. 34.
2 *Toronto Mail,* July 9, 1892.
3 *Parry Sound North Star,* September 19, 1897.
4 Ada Florence Kinton. *Just One Blue Bonnet, The Life Story of Ada Florence Kinton,* (1907). p. 34.
5 *From Muskoka & Haliburton 1615-1875.* Edited by Florence B. Murray. The Champlain Society for the Government of Ontario, University of Toronto Press, 1963) p. 125.
6 *Toronto Mail,* July 9, 1892.
7 *Ibid.*

CHAPTER 2 THE UNKNOWN

1 Rev. John S. Firmin. *Other Places, Parry Sound District. Chapman, Armour, Ryerson and Strong Townships.* (unpublished, c. 1977 File VII, West Parry Sound Public Library Archives).
2 *Ibid.*
3 *Ibid.*
4 John F. Hayes. "Tales of the Early Days," (unpublished collection of papers, 1967). Sundridge-Strong Union Public Library Archives. p. 87.
5 *Ibid.*
6 Rev. John S. Firmin. *Other Places, Parry Sound District, Spence,Chapman, Armour, Ryerson and Strong Townships.* (c. 1967).
7 *Ibid.*
8 *Toronto Mail,* July 30, 1892.
9 *Powassan News,* May 16, 1951.
10 "Ernie Richardson's Memoirs." (unpublished, Nipissing Museum Collection, 1959, updated 1964). Not paginated.
11 *Parry Sound North Star,* April 18, 1879.

CHAPTER 3 JOHN SAMPSON SCARLETT

1 "Algoma Anglican." Stuart Lindsay-Hoback, Port Sydney Christ Church, May 1996.
2 George W. Beyer. *Early Days in Muskoka,* (Bracebridge, Herald-Gazette Press, 1970). p. 257
3 *Toronto Mail,* July 9, 1892.
4 *The Lake in the Hills, Strong Township and Sundridge, 1875-1925.* Edited by Alice May Robins, compiled by Patricia Lee. (Cobalt, Highway Book Store, 1989) p. 185.
5 John F. Hayes. "Tales of the Early Days," (unpublished collection of papers, 1967) Sundridge-Strong Union Public Library Archives, p. 185
6 Rev. John S. Firmin. *Other Places, Parry Sound District, Spence, Chapman, Armour, Ryerson and Strong Townships,* (unpublished, c. 1977, File V11, West Parry Sound Public Library Archives). Not paginated.
7 *Toronto Mail,* Saturday, July 9, 1892.
8 *Parry Sound North Star,* January 16, 1885.
9 *Powassan News,* May 2, 1951.
10 *Ibid.*
11 *Ibid.*
12 *Parry Sound North Star,* March 6, 1885.
13 "Algoma Anglican." Stuart Lindsay-Hoback. May 1996.

CHAPTER 4 THE SCOTIA JUNCTION DIFFICULTY

1 Tweedsmuire Village History, Book I. "Introduction." Emsdale-Scotia Women's Institute. Not paginated.
2 Allan Bell. *A Way to the West—A Canadian Railway Legend,* (Barrie, Ontario. Privately published, 1991). Appendix A. p. 157.
3 *Ibid.* Pp. 58-9.
4 *Almaguin News,* April 27, 1967.
5 Allan Bell. *A Way to the West—A Canadian Railway Legend* (1991). p. 70.
6 *Ibid.* p. 3.
7 *Almaguin News,* April 27, 1967.
8 Allan Bell. *A Way to the West—A Canadian Railway Legend.* (1991). p. 157.

9   *Parry Sound North Star,* March 17, 1898.

10 *Ibid.* December 15, 1898.

11 *Ibid.* March 17, 1898.

12 *Ibid.* December 15, 1898.

13 *Ibid.* December 15, 1898.

14 *Ibid.* December 15, 1898.

15 *Almaguin News,* April 27, 1967.

16 Allan Bell. *A Way to the West—A Canadian Railway Legend.* (1991). p. 126.

17 *bid.* p. 126.

18 *Ibid.* p. 144.

19 *Almaguin News,* April 27, 1967.

CHAPTER 5 MURDER AT EMSDALE

1   Tweedsmuire Village History, Book 2. Emsdale-Scotia Women's Institute. "An interview of William Acton." Not paginated.

2   *Parry Sound North Star,* March 27, 1885.

3   *Ibid.*

4   *Ibid.*

CHAPTER 6 THE HIGHLANDER AND THE TEMPERANCE MOVEMENT

1   *Sprucedale Banner Parry Sound North Star,* March 14, 1907.

2   *Ibid.* May 9, 1907

3   Jim Lotz (Ed.). *Prime Ministers of Canada.* (London, England, Bison Books, 1987) p. 18-19.

4   *Sprucedale Banner, Parry Sound North Star,* March 21, 1907.

5   *Ibid.* May 9, 1907.

6   George W. Boyer. *Early Days in Muskoka.* (Bracebridge, Herald-Gazette Press, 1970). p. 12.

7   *Ibid.* p. 12.

8   *Parry Sound North Star,* August 22, 1879.

9   *Sprucedale Banner, Parry Sound North Star,* May 9, 1907.

10 *Parry Sound North Star,* February 16, 1889.

11 *Parry Sound North Star,* April 13, 1889.

12 Janice Madill. *A Tract Through Time.* (Sprucedale, Township of McMurrich, Olympic Printing, 1994). p. 243.

13 *Ibid.* Pp. 27-29.

CHAPTER 7 DAVID FRANCIS BURK

1   *From Muskoka & Haliburton 1615-1875.* Edited by Florence B. Murray. "Up The Muskoka and Down The Trent" The Champlain Society for the Government of Ontario, (University of Toronto Press, 1963). p. 393.

2   *Toronto Globe,* October 4, 1865.

3   *From Muskoka & Haliburton 1615-1875.* (1963). p. 393.

4   *Ibid.*

5   *Oshawa Times,* November 3, 1984.

6   *Almaguin News,* July 7, 1976.

7   *Oshawa Times,* November 3, 1984.

CHAPTER 8 ENROUTE TO BURK'S FALLS

1   *Just One Blue Bonnet, The Life Story of Ada Florence Kinton.* Edited by her sister, Sara A. Randleson. (Toronto, William Briggs, 1907). p. 54-55.

2   *Memories of Burk's Falls and District, 1835-1978.* (Village of Burk's Falls) 1978, p. 9.

3   *Just One Blue Bonnet, The Life Story of Ada Florence Kinton.* (1907). p 54-55.

4   *Ibid.*

5   Interview with Harold Todd, Novar. July 27, 1996.

6   *Just One Blue Bonnet, The Life Story of Ada Florence Kinton.*(1907). p 54-55.

7   *Ibid.*

8   Interview with Harold Todd, Novar, July 27, 1996.

9   *Burk's Falls Arrow and Sundridge Echo,* February 6, 1964.

10 *Just One Blue Bonnet, The Life Story of Ada Florence Kinton.* (1907). p 56.

11 *Ibid.*

12 *Ibid.*

13 *Ibid.*

CHAPTER 9 JAMES SHARPE: AN ORIGINAL

1   *Parry Sound North Star,* August 22, 1879.

2   *Toronto Mail,* July 30, 1892.

3   *Parry Sound North Star,* October 2, 1885.

4   Rev. John S. Firmin. *Other Places, Parry Sound District, Spence, Chapman, Armour, Ryerson and Strong Townships.* (unpublished, c. 1977, File V11) West Parry Sound Public Library Archives. p 40-41.

5   *Toronto Mail,* July 30, 1892.

6   *Toronto Mail,* July 9, 1892.

7   Rev. John S. Firmin. *Other Places, Parry Sound District, Spence, Chapman, Armour, Ryerson and Strong Townships.* (c. 1977). p 40-41.

8   *Ibid.*

9   *Ibid.*

10 *Ibid.*

CHAPTER 10 TROUBLE AT THE BURK'S FALLS BEACON!

1 *Parry Sound North Star*, September 22, 1898.
2 *Ibid.*
3 *Ibid.*
4 *Ibid.*

CHAPTER 11 THE GREAT PINE LOG MYSTERY

1 *Almaguin News*, July 1973.
2 *Yours For Fun* Summer Magazine (*Almaguin News*) 1994.

CHAPTER 12 ANGUS KENNEDY 'LONG LIVE HE'

1 *Cawthra Scrapbooks* (private collection, Jane Gavine, Burk's Falls).
2 *Burk's Falls Arrow*, May 10, 1951.
3 *Cawthra Scrapbooks*
4 *The Lake in the Hills, Strong Township and Sundridge, 1875-1925.* Edited by Alice May Robins, compiled by Patricia Lee, (Cobalt, Highway Book Store, 1989) p. 52.
5 *Ibid.*
6 *Toronto Mail*, July 9, 1892.
7 *Ibid.*
8 *The Lake in the Hills, Strong Township and Sundridge, 1875-1925.* (1989) p. 52.
9 *Cawthra Scrapbooks.*
10 *Burk's Falls Arrow*, May 10, 1951.
11 *Ibid.*
12 *Parry Sound North Star*, November 15, 1905.
13 *Burk's Falls Arrow*, May 10, 1951.
14 *Ibid.*
15 *Ibid*
16 *Cawthra Scrapbooks.*

CHAPTER 13 AN ILL WIND

1 *Parry Sound North Star*, June 25, 1908.
2 *Ibid.*
3 *Ibid.*
4 *Almaguin News*, July 21, 1976.
5 *Burk's Falls Arrow*, May 10, 1951.
6 *Toronto Mail*, Saturday, July 30, 1892.
7 *Parry Sound North Star*, June 25, 1908. (additional reading, *Reflections of a Century, Burk's Falls 1890-1990.* Sprucedale, Olympic Printing, 1990). p. 23.
8 *Parry Sound North Star*, March 1, 1905.
9 *Parry Sound North Star*, April 16, 1908.

CHAPTER 14 DICK THE BUMMER

1 Rev. John S. Firmin. *Other Places, Parry Sound District, Spence, Chapman, Armour, Ryerson and Strong Townships.* (unpublished, c. 1977, File V11, West Parry Sound Public Library archives). Not paginated.
2 *Almaguin News*, Obituary of Edmund Russell, January 25, 1967.
3 Rev. John S. Firmin. *Other Places, Parry Sound District, Spence, Chapman, Armour, Ryerson and Strong Townships.* (c. 1977). Not paginated.

CHAPTER 15 DARK DOINGS AT DUFFERIN

1 *Parry Sound NorthStar*, May 9, 1879.
2 *Parry Sound North Star*, July 18, 1879.
3 *Parry Sound North Star*, August 8, 1879.
4 *Ibid.*
5 *Parry Sound North Star*, September 8, 1879.
6 *Parry Sound North Star*, August 22, 1879.
7 *Ibid.*
8 *Parry Sound North Star*, August 8, 1879.
9 *Parry Sound North Star*, August 22, 1879.
10 *Parry Sound North Star*, October 21, 1879.
11 *Parry Sound North Star*, October 21, 1879.
12 Ron Brown, *Ghost Towns of Ontario* Volume 1, (Toronto, Canon Books, 1990). p. 92.
13 *Morry's Directory 1901 Local History: The Union Publishing Co. of Ingersoll—Farmers and Business Directory for the counties of Durham, Haliburton, Northumberland, Peterborough, and Victoria and the Districts of Muskoka, Nipissing, Parry Sound, Algoma and Manitoulin.* Vol XII (issued biannually).
14 *Almaguin News*, April 5, 1995.

CHAPTER 16 THE TWELFTH OF JULY

1 *Almaguin News*, July 20, 1967.
2 *Parry Sound North Star*, July 24, 1885.
3 *Almaguin News*, July 20, 1967.
4 *Burk's Falls Arrow & Sundridge Echo*, (publication date unknown, author unknown).
5 *Cawthra Scrapbooks*, (private collection, Jane Garvine, Burk's Falls).

CHAPTER 17 CAT FAMINE

1 *Parry Sound North Star*, March 2, 1889.
2 *Ibid.*

3   *The Lake in the Hills, Strong Township and Sundridge, 1875-1925.* Edited by Alice May Robins, compiled by Patricia Lee. (Cobalt, Highway Book Store, 1989).

4   *Parry Sound North Star,* March 2, 1889.

5   *Ibid.*

6   *Ibid.*

CHAPTER 18 THE MAGNETAWAN RIVER

1   *Burk's Falls Arrow* & *Sundridge Echo,* July 6, 1966.

2   *Ibid.*

3   *Ibid.*

4   Rev. John S. Firmin. *Other Places, Parry Sound District, Spence, Chapman, Armour, Ryerson and Strong Townships.* (unpublished, c. 1977, File V11, West Parry Sound Library archives). Not paginated.

5   *Parry Sound North Star,* Oct. 2, 1885.

6   *Burk's Falls Arrow* & *Sundridge Echo,* July 6, 1966.

7   *Ibid.*

8   *Ibid.*

9   *Ibid.*

10 *Ibid.*

11 *Burk's Falls Arrow* & *Sundridge Echo,* August 24, 1966.

12 Rev. John S. Firmin. *Other Places, Parry Sound District, Spence, Chapman, Armour, Ryerson and Strong Townships.* (c. 1977). Not paginated.

CHAPTER 19 ERA OF THE RIVER DRIVES

1   *Burk's Falls Arrow* & *Sundridge Echo,* July 13, 1966. (reprinted from the *Toronto Globe* c. 1930).

2   *Ibid.*

3   Rev. John S. Firmin. *Other Places, Parry Sound District, Spence, Chapman, Armour, Ryerson and Strong Townships.* (unpublished, c. 1977, File V11, West Parry Sound Public Library archives.) Not paginated.

4   *Burk's Falls Arrow* & *Sundridge Echo,* August 3, 1966.

5   *Guide Book and Atlas of Muskoka and Parry Sound Districts.* References not available.

6   *Burk's Falls Arrow and Sundridge Echo,* August 24, 1966.

7   Rev. John S. Firmin. *Other Places, Parry Sound District, Spence, Chapman, Armour, Ryerson and Strong Townships.* (c. 1977).

8   *Ibid.*

9   *Ibid.*

10 *Burk's Falls Arrow* & *Sundridge Echo,* August 24, 1956.

11 *Ibid.*

12 Rev. John S. Firmin. *Other Places, Parry Sound District, Spence, Chapman, Armour, Ryerson and Strong Townships.* (c. 1977).

13 Daley Bros. of Magnetawan plant records (courtesy of Marilyn Raaflaub).

14 *Burk's Falls Arrow and Sundridge Echo,* August 24, 1956.

15 Daley Bros. of Magnetawan plant records.

16 *Burk's Falls Arrow* & *Sundridge Echo,* July 13, 1966. (reprinted from the *Toronto Globe* c. 1930).

17 *Ibid.*

CHAPTER 20 LUMBERJACKS

1   John Macfie. *Now and Then, Footnotes to Parry Sound History* (Parry Sound, Georgian Bay Beacon Publishing Co. Ltd., 1983). p. 93.

2   *Burk's Falls Arrow and Sundridge Echo,* May 10, 1951.

3   *Ibid.*

4   *Ibid.*

5   John Macfie. *Now and Then Footnotes to Parry Sound History.* (1983). p. 51.

6   *Ibid.*

7   John F. Hayes. "Tales of the Early Days." (unpublished collection of papers Sundridge-Strong Union Public Library archives, 1967). p. 15.

8   *Ibid.*

9   *Just One Blue Bonnet, The Life Story of Ada Florence Kinton.* Edited by her sister, Sara A. Randleson. (Toronto, William Briggs, 1907). p. 56.

10 *Burk's Falls Arrow and Sundrdige Echo,* May 10, 1951.

11 John Macfie. *Now and Then, Footnotes to Parry Sound History* (1983). p. 142.

12 *Just One Blue Bonnet, The Life Story of Ada Florence Kinton.* (1907). p. 57.

13 *Ibid.*

14 *Ibid.*

15 John Macfie. *Now and Then, Footnotes to Parry Sound History.* (1983). p. 69.

16 *Ibid.*

17 *Powassan News,* June 20, 1951.

18 *Ibid.*

CHAPTER 21 THE SAWMILL WAS FIRST

1   *Almaguin News,* February 9, 1972.

2   *Ibid.*

3   *Ibid.*

4   *Almaguin News,* May 11, 1967.

5   *Almaguin News,* February 9, 1972.

6   *Burk's Falls Arrow & Sundridge Echo*, March 28, 1964.
7   *Almaguin News*, February 9, 1972.
8   *Ibid.*
9   *Burk's Falls Arrow & Sundridge Echo*, March 28, 1964.
10 *Ibid.*
11 *Almaguin News*, February 9, 1972.
12 *Almaguin News*, February 16, 1972.
13 *Almaguin News*, May 25, 1967.

CHAPTER 22 POWASSAN: A BEND IN THE RIVER

1   *Powassan News*, July 9, 1952.
2   *Ibid.*
3   *Ibid.*
4   *Powassan News*, May 7, 1952.
5   *Powassan News*, April 11, 1951.
6   *Burk's Falls Arrow & Sundridge Echo*, November 30, 1966.
7   *Powassan News*, April 11, 1951.
8   *Burk's Falls Arrow & Sundridge Echo*, November 30, 1966.
9   *Powassan News*, April 11, 1951.
10 *Burk's Falls Arrow & Sundridge Echo*, November 30, 1966.
11 *Ibid.*
12 *Ibid.*
13 *Powassan News*, July 9, 1952.
14 *Powassan News*, April 11, 1951.
15 *Ibid.*
16 *Burk's Falls Arrow &Sundridge Echo*, November 30, 1966.
17 *Ibid.*
18 *Ibid.*
19 *Powassan News*, April 11, 1951.
20 *Ibid.*

CHAPTER 23 FISH TALES

1   *Almaguin News*, January 21, 1976.
2   *Ibid.*
3   *Ibid.*
4   *Ibid.*
5   *Powassan News*, May 23, 1951.
6   *Ibid.*
7   *Ibid.*
8   *Ibid.*
9   *Ibid.*

CHAPTER 24 MOOSE TALES: A HUNT AND A STAMPEDE

1   *Powassan News*, May 7, 1952.
2   *Ibid.*
3   *Ibid.*
4   *Ibid.*
5   *Ibid.*
6   *Powassan News*, May 23, 1951.
7   *Ibid.*
8   *Ibid.*
9   *Ibid.*

CHAPTER 25 THE OLD MOOSE TRAIL: SO THE STORY GOES

1   *Powassan News*, August 1, 1951.
2   *Powassan News*, June 6, 1951.
3   *Powassan News*, June 13, 1951.
4   *Powassan News*, August 1, 1951.
5   *Ibid.*
6   *Ibid.*
7   *Ibid.*
8   *Ibid.*
9   *Ibid.*
10 *Ibid.*

CHAPTER 26 NIPISSING VILLAGE

1   *Almaguin News*, August 7, 1974.
2   *Almaguin News*, October 11, 1995.
3   "Ernie Richardson Memoirs" (unpublished, Nipissing Museum Archives. 1959: updated 1964). Not paginated.
4   *Ibid.*
5   *Ibid.*
6   *Almaguin News*, October 1, 1975.
7   *Pioneer Days in the Township of Nipissing*. A Township of Nipissing Publication, (Callander, Ontario, Hamilton Printers, 1974). p. 9.
8   *Almaguin News*, October 1, 1975.
9   *Ibid.*
10 *Pioneer Days in the Township of Nipissing*. (1974). p. 24.
11 "Ernie Richardson Memoirs" (1959: updated 1964). Not paginated.
12 *Ibid*
13 *Burk's Falls Arrow and Sundridge Echo*, November 30, 1966.

14 "Ernie Richardson Memoirs."

15 *Ibid.*

16 *Ibid.*

17 *Almaguin News*, March 1974.

18 *Almaguin News*, December, 1973.

CHAPTER 27 THE STAGECOACH STOPPED HERE

1 Conversations with Ralph Bice, during the spring of 1988.

2 *Ibid.*

CHAPTER 28 THE MAWS OF RESTOULE

1 *Mail & Empire*, Toronto, July 7 1922 and *Evening Telegram*, Toronto, July 7, 1922.

2 June (McVeety) Hampel. *Reflections of Restoule 1850-1991*. (Aylmer, *Aylmer Express Ltd.* 1991.) p. 115, 137.

3 *Ibid.*

4 *Mail & Empire*, Toronto, July 7, 1922 and *Evening Telegram*, Toronto, July 7, 1922.

5 *Ibid.*

6 Telephone conversations with Elizabeth Marchant Maw-Cockeram (before her death in July, 1996) during the fall of 1995.

7 *Toronto Telegram*, June 16, 1949.

8 Conversation with Elizabeth Maw-Cockeram's son David Plumb and daughter-in-law Judith Diehl, during the fall of 1997.

CHAPTER 29 THE BRIDGE THAT WILL LAST FOREVER

1 *Cawthra Scrapbooks* (private collection, Jane Gavine, Burk's Falls).

CHAPTER 30 PERSONALITIES OF TODAY

1 Conversations with Peter Carmani, during the winter of 1997.

2 *Ibid.*

3 *Ibid.*

4 *Ibid.*

5 *Almaguin News*, January 22, 1992.

6 Conversations with Sandy Coombs during the winter of 1997.

7 *Almaguin News*, January 22, 1992.

8 *Almaguin News*, June 14, 1995.

9 *Almaguin News*, October 29, 1997.

10 *Ibid.*

11 Conversations with Doug Mackey during the winter of 1997.

12 Conversations with Mike McIntosh during the winter of 1997.

13 *Ibid.*

14 *From Forest To Pharmacy: Canada's Underground Trade in Bear Parts*. A Report by the Investigative Network for The Humane Society of the United States/Humane Society International, The Humane Society of Canada. Peter Knights and Sue Fisher. 1995, p. 1.

15 Conversations with Muriel Parker during the winter in 1997.

16 *Ibid.*

17 *Ibid.*

18 *Ibid.*

19 *Ibid.*

20 *Ibid.*

21 *Ibid.*

CHAPTER 31 GONE BUT NOT FORGOTTEN

1 *Almaguin News,* May 14, 1976.

2 *Ibid.*

3 *Burk's Falls Arrow & Sundridge Echo,* November 2, 1966.

4 *Burk's Falls Arrow & Sundridge Echo,* June 15, 1966.

5 Conversations with John (Jack) Trussler during the winter of 1997.

6 Ralph Bice, *Along The Trail in Algonquin Park*. (Toronto, Natural Heritage Books [1980, 1981] 1993) p. 23.

7 *Toronto Star,* Obituary, August 26, 1997.

8 "Field Notes," a column by the outdoor writer Gary Ball. (Source not available.)

9 Conversations with Marilyn (Bice) MacKay during September and December of 1997, spring of 1998.

10 Ralph Bice, *Along The Trail in Algonquin Park* (1993) p. 24.

Bibliography

A Way to the West-A Canadian Railway Legend. Allan Bell. (Barrie, Ontario, privately published) 1991.

"Algoma Anglican." Stuart Lindsay-Hoback (Port Sydney Christ Church.) May 1996.

Along the Trail in Algonquin Park. Ralph Bice (Toronto, Natural Heritage Books) 1993.

Early Days in Muskoka. (Bracebridge, Herald Gazette Press) 1970.

"Ernie Richardson Memoirs." (Unpublished, Nipissing Museum Collection) 1959, updated 1964.

From Muskoka & Haliburton 1615-1875 . Florence B. Murray, Editor. (The Champlain Society for the Government of Canada, University of Toronto Press) 1907.

Ghost Towns of Ontario. Vol. 1. Ron Brown (Toronto, Cannon Books) 1990.

Just One Blue Bonnet, The Life Story of Ada Florence Kinton.. Ada Florence Kinton. Edited by Sara A. Randleson. (Toronto, William Briggs) 1907.

Memories of Burk's Falls and District, 1835-1978 (Village of Burk's Falls) 1978.

Now and Then, Footnotes to Parry Sound History. John Macfie (Parry Sound, Georgian Bay Beacon Publishing Co. Ltd.) 1983.

Other Places, Parry Sound District: Chapman, Armour, Ryerson and Strong Townships. Rev. John S. Firmin (Unpublished File VII, Parry Sound Public Library Archives) c.1977.

Pioneer Days in Township of Nipissing. A Township of Nipissing Publication (Callender, Hamilton Printers) 1974.

Prime Ministers of Canada. Jim Lotz, Ed. (London, England, Bison Books) 1987.

Reflections of Restoule. June (McVeety) Hampel (Aylmer, Aylmer Express Ltd.) 1991.

"Tales of the Early Days." John F. Hayes (unpublished papers, Sundridge-Strong Union Library Archives) 1967.

The Lake in the Hills, Strong Township and Sundridge, 1875-1925. Alice May Robins Ed., compiled by Patricia Lee. (Cobalt, Highway Book Store) 1989.

Photo Credits

COVER

Background photo. Courtesy the author

Top photo. Original glass negative, courtesy Carmen Maeck. Photograph courtesy the South River-Macar Union Public Library

Bottom photo. Courtesy Archives of Ontario, c. 120-3, 55163

BACK COVER

Fawn photo. Courtesy Mike McIntosh

Moose photo. Courtesy Marilyn (Bice) MacKay

FRONTISPIECE

Loading logs on the Trout Creek Logging Railroad 1915. Courtesy John (Jack) Trussler

CHAPTER 1 SETTLING THE NEW LAND

Settler's Shanty. Etching by author.

Log Cabin. Courtesy the Archives of Ontario— ACC6287 S8248.

CHAPTER 4 THE SCOTIA JUNCTION DIFFICULTY

Scotia Junction Railway Station. Courtesy Ron and Ethel Thornton of Kearney.

Scotia Junction Railway Station, 1914. Courtesy Tweedsmuire Village History, Emsdale-Scotia Women's Institute.

The Last Steamer. Courtesy Tweedsmuire Village History, Emsdale-Scotia Women's Institute.

The Albion Hotel. Courtesy Tweedsmuire Village History, Emsdale-Scotia Women's Institute.

Railway Hotel Dining Room. Courtesy Tweedsmuire Village History, Emsdale-Scotia Women's Institute.

Scotia Main Street. Courtesy Tweedsmuire Village History, Emsdale-Scotia Women's Institute.

CHAPTER 5 MURDER AT EMSDALE

The Maples on Star Lake Road. Courtesy Tweedsmuire Village History, Emsdale-Scotia Women's Institute.

South Church Street in Emsdale. Courtesy Tweedsmuire Village History, Emsdale-Scotia Women's Institute.

The Perry Township Agricultural Society. Courtesy Tweedsmuire Village History, Emsdale-Scotia Women's Institute.

CHAPTER 6 THE HIGHLANDER AND THE TEMPERANCE MOVEMENT

The *Nipissing* Sidewheeler. Courtesy the Archives of Ontario, F1132-2-1 ST1213.

CHAPTER 8 ENROUTE TO BURK'S FALLS

Old postcard. Courtesy Betty Caldwell

CHAPTER 11 THE GREAT PINE LOG MYSTERY

Log Shanty. Pencil sketch by author.

CHAPTER 12 ANGUS KENNEDY 'LONG LIVE HE'

Community gathering at Burk's Falls. Courtesy *Almaguin News*.

CHAPTER 13 AN ILL WIND

View of the South-east side. Courtesy Betty Caldwell.

Surviving Business Buildings. Courtesy Betty Caldwell.

CHAPTER 15 DARK DOINGS AT DUFFERIN

Morden family tombstone. Photo by the author.

CHAPTER 18 THE ALMAGUIN RIVER

Wanita, Armour and *Gravenhurst* steamers. Courtesy Betty Caldwell.

Summer Picnic. Courtesy Betty Caldwell.

CHAPTER 19 ERA OF THE RIVER DRIVES

General Store. Original glass negative, Carmen Maeck. Courtesy South River-Machar Union Public Library

CHAPTER 20 LUMBERJACKS

Farmers employed by the big logging company. Courtesy Archives of Ontario C120-3, 55163.

CHAPTER 21 THE SAWMILL WAS FIRST

Glen Roberts Tea Room. Photo by author. Courtesy *Almaguin News*.
Trout Creek Store Co. Courtesy John (Jack) Trussler
Trussler Bros. Logging Road. Courtesy John (Jack) Trussler
Trout Creek Heisler Locomotive. Courtesy John (Jack) Trussler
Trussler Bros. Mill. Courtesy John (Jack) Trussler
Rosseau-Nipissing Colonization Road. Photo by author.
Hauling Logs for the Dominion Wood and Chemical Gas Plant. Courtesy John (Jack) Trussler

CHAPTER 22 POWASSAN: A BEND IN THE RIVER

191 King Street, John Sampson Scarlett's store. Photo by author.
Demolition of the roundbuilding. Photo by author. Courtesy *Almaguin News*.

CHAPTER 23 FISH TALES

Trout Catch. Courtesy Marilyn (Bice) MacKay.

CHAPTER 25 THE OLD MOOSE TRAIL: SO THE STORY GOES

Commanda Museum Tourist Shop. Photo by author.
Commanda Museum. Photo by author.

CHAPTER 26 NIPISSING VILLAGE

Richardson & Bros. General Store. Courtesy Archives of Ontario, ACC9258 S14338.
Nipissing Hotel. Courtesy Archives of Ontario ACC9258 S14325.

CHAPTER 27 THE STAGECOACH STOPPED HERE

Sunset Haven. Photo by author. Courtesy *The Weekend-Almaguin News*.

CHAPTER 28 THE MAWS OF RESTOULE

The Maw family relaxing by the shores of Homewood Island. Courtesy David Plumb.
Camping out in tents. Courtesy David Plumb.
Maw family cottage. Courtesy David Plumb.
Grawbarger Rapid Chute. Courtesy David Plumb.

CHAPTER 29 THE BRIDGE THAT WILL STAND FOREVER

Galna Bridge. Courtesy Betty Caldwell.

CHAPTER 30 PERSONALITIES OF TODAY

Peter Camani's mediaeval home. Photo by author. Courtesy *Almaguin News*.
Sandy Coombs, Reeve of the village of Magnetawan. Photo by author.
Camp-in at the Magnetawan lock. Courtesy *Almaguin News*.
Lock construction. Photo by author. Courtesy *Almaguin News*.
Rural Watch, Doug Mackey. Courtesy *Almaguin News*.
Mike McIntosh with 'Freddie'. Photo by author.
Black bears playing in field. Photo by author. Courtesy *Almaguin News*.
Muriel Parker with Girl Guides. Photo by author. Courtesy *Almaguin News*.

CHAPTER 31 GONE BUT NOT FORGOTTEN

Trussler School. Courtesy John (Jack) Trussler.
Trussler Bros. mill at Trout Creek. Courtesy John (Jack) Trussler.
Ralph Bice as a young man. Courtesy Marilyn (Bice) MacKay.
Ralph Bice in his cabin. Courtesy Marilyn (Bice) MacKay.
Ralph in a fur hat. Courtesy Marilyn (Bice) MacKay.

Index

ABOUT THE AUTHOR

Although a city girl, born in Toronto, as a child Astrid spent most of her summers at the family's summer residence in the District of Parry Sound. The cabin was, and still is, located on Compass Lake in McMurrich Township (now McMurrich/Montieth Township). Those memorable summers spent with her parents were to leave a lasting impression. A first generation Canadian, Astrid very quickly learned to appreciate the Almaguin Highlands as the region reminded her parents, refugees from the Second World War of their homeland, Estonia.

While attending university, she became involved with the grassroots conservation group, the Local Architectural Conservation Advisory Committee (LACAC), and soon became their historical researcher for the Town of Markham. At the same time, Astrid became a regular columnist with the weekly *Markham Economist and Sun*, writing about the history of the early settlers of Markham. After graduating from the University of Toronto's Victoria College, specializing in fine art and architecture, Astrid went on to spend a year at Toronto's Ontario College of Art (OCA), perfecting her printmaking skills.

Before joining the editorial staff at the *Almaguin News* in 1988, Astrid spent a number of years as a district correspondent with the *North Bay Nugget*. Today, she makes her home in Burk's Falls, where as well as writing, Astrid lends her support to environmental and humane causes.